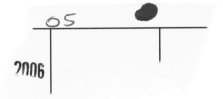
HOT EARTH COLD EARTH

Books by James Berry

POETRY

Fractured Circles (New Beacon Books, 1979)
Lucy's Letters and Loving (New Beacon Books, 1982)
Chain of Days (Oxford University Press, 1985)
Hot Earth Cold Earth (Bloodaxe Books, 1995)

ANTHOLOGIES

Bluefoot Traveller (Limestone Publications, 1976;
 revised edition, Nelson, 1985)
News for Babylon (Chatto & Windus, 1984;
 new edition, Bloodaxe Books, 1996)
Dance to a different drum (Brixton Community Festival, 1983)
Classic Poems to Read Aloud (Kingfisher, 1995)

BOOKS FOR CHILDREN

A Thief in the Village (Hamish Hamilton, 1987)
The Girls and Yanga Marshall: four stories (Longman, 1987)
When I Dance (Hamish Hamilton, 1988)
Anancy-Spiderman (Walker Books, 1988)
Isn't My Name Magical? (Longman/BBC, 1990)
The Future-Telling Lady (Hamish Hamilton, 1991)
Ajeemah and His Son, novella (HarperCollins, 1992)
Celebration Song (Hamish Hamilton, 1994)
Playing a Dazzler (Hamish Hamilton, 1996)
Don't Leave an Elephant to Chase a Bird (Simon & Schuster, 1996)

JAMES BERRY

HOT EARTH
COLD EARTH

BLOODAXE BOOKS

Copyright © James Berry 1985, 1995

ISBN: 1 85224 330 9

First published 1995 by
Bloodaxe Books Ltd,
P.O. Box 1SN,
Newcastle upon Tyne NE99 1SN.

Bloodaxe Books Ltd acknowledges
the financial assistance of Northern Arts.

To the memory of my mother and father
MAUD & ROBERT BERRY

Cover printing by J. Thomson Colour Printers Ltd, Glasgow.

Printed in Great Britain by
Cromwell Press Ltd, Broughton Gifford, Melksham, Wiltshire.

CONTENTS

ACKNOWLEDGEMENTS

The poems in the last section of this book are selected from *Chain of Days*, originally published by Oxford University Press in 1985.

Acknowledgements are due to the editors of the following publications in which some of the new poems first appeared: *Ambit, Bluefoot Traveller* (Nelson, 1985), *Chapman, Hinterland: Caribbean Poetry from the West Indies & Britain* (Bloodaxe Books, 1989), *The New British Poetry* (Paladin, 1988), *New Statesman & Society, Poetry* (Chicago), *Poetry Review, Poetry Book Society Anthology 1987-1988* (PBS/Hutchinson, 1987), *South East Arts Review, Tiano Covering Columbus* (Panrun, 1992) and *With a Poet's Eye* (Tate Gallery, 1986).

The cover painting is *The Migration Series* (1940-41) Panel #7 by Jacob Lawrence. The caption to this painting reads: 'The migrant, whose life had been rural and nurtured by the earth, was now moving to urban life dependent on industrial machinery' (title and text revised by the artist, 1993). Casein tempera on hardboard, The Phillips Collection, Washington, DC.

PREFACE

Hot Earth Cold Earth is a book of new poems with some collected from a previous book, *Chain of Days*, now out of print.

Looking at the new poems, and the obsessions they reflect, I feel that sharing some background information may well assist the reader. One poem in particular prompted this feeling, 'My Letter to You, Mother Africa'.

Personal discoveries, from when I was young at school, gradually revealed a sense that as a black child I was born into an imprisoned people. I began to see I suffered the lacks of my family. From about eight or nine years old I began to notice how the ex-slave-owners' descendants of my village treated my father automatically as an inferior. And my father accepted his position, as if it was all in the way of things. A terror settled in me that I was placed to grow up into my father's position. Inward, thoughtful, anxious, desperate to read books nobody had, I lived with the dread that lack of money and education and opportunity would condemn me to repeat that same design of life impressed upon my ancestors up to my father.

Shelley's line 'I fall upon the thorns of life! I bleed!' could describe the silent state of mind in a continuing pain that gathered itself and became 'Letter to Mother Africa'.

I had seen and understood that nobody liked Africa. Yet, it was much later I realised I knew and understood nothing positive about Africa and Africans. At school Africa embarrassed us and stirred us with a sense of shame, like slavery did. Our feelings for Africa aroused more horror and dread and hatred than any curiosity.

An impelling need grew in me. Mentally, I needed to go back to my African roots with my hurt, anger and a complaining voice. My state of mind became fixed on addressing my ancestral country, continent and rulership, as to a child-abandoning mother.

Equality meant shouldering a share of responsibility. I wanted Mother Africa to voice acknowledging a share of responsibility for the under-human and outsider status that was allowed to be implanted into the life and being of African descendants in Western society.

I lived in America. I lived in England. My experience broadened. I saw that the devouring, grasping and warring instincts of a group's self-love could not change or even be modified by itself without demands made by others. The obviously poor and poverty-stricken were evident as fixtures. But the illiteracies and human lacks of the "best educated" and privileged people, who ran our world and dispensed its resources, were all well hidden, suavely and urbanely camouflaged, as non-existent.

Yet, there were seeming unconscious drives to unite the world as one jointly unified responsibility. And in that black people obviously had the most difficult part. To most white people, the mere presence of a black person aroused a symbolism of a dreaded "dark" and "black" menace. And that was coupled with that basic separatist tribal nature of human groups.

I had to wait for a reply to my letter, and search for its arrival. And when 'Reply from Mother Africa' came, its contents were a surprise.

Now looking at the chronicled order of these poems, I recognise each stage as part of an emotional map. And, as you yourself will notice, in spite of the shocks and howlings of a culture-crossing, celebration is neither missing nor drowned.

JAMES BERRY

ONE

Spirits of Movement

Surely, so alike, airborne wind gave birth
to water, issued the denser wash
and earthed the early offspring.

Inbuilt is wind-inheritance.
Rage of leaves resists face-wash
it is wind's arrival in trees.

Hear sea waves work-choir,
hear any waterfall wonder,
its temple-roar of wind flooding woods.

A restless transparent busyness
going and going. Spirits of movement.
Both break all shores, mad mad in search.

Wind plays wild bands of ghosts.
Water organises running river
and drives rain-floods hustling.

On any sitting duty
like being a pond or puddle,
canal or glassful

water waits to run away
or just disappear like wind.
In a settled state water is sad.

Drop a stone in a sleepy pool
you hear the sulk
of static water voiced.

Lock up water, give it time, it'll leave.
Drink it down, it presses wanting exit.
A job done, water vanishes.

Water'll freshen any body part
and be ready, hanging
in drips, to be off.

Does its work, yes. But to be
ungraspable, like wind,
water insists on its transfiguration.

Haiku Moments: 1

1

The sea-sound sunlight –
pinnate leaves of palms rattle
a lost young bird cries.

2

The humming bird sucks
the open red hibiscus
fluttering its leaves.

3

Hill tree staged parrots
woodpecker screams in the noon
stream pours into self.

4

The frogs are croaking
fireflies wink together
darkness drips rainfall.

Hot Day Before My Time

Scent of blossom
scent of blossom them have tipsy bees a-dawdle,
sun face a-drip it dazzle.
Collect hot earth creation them from sunhot:
bag them up, bag up a nation market lot.

Mortar pound
mortar pound roast coffee
like cassava fo bammy,
cocobeans fo chocolate,
corn fo cornpone
and make dog ketch a bone.

Mango a-ripe, mango a-ripe,
bird them in a branch full a fight.
Breadfruit fatten up cut hog,
spiced pork sizzle fo dogwood log.

Hen lay egg, hen a-cackle:
mongoose know whey to get a suckle.
A banana-day, man, a banana pay
come bubble up in a rum day.

cut hog: castrated pig.

A People Gone

I see you much more keenly now, first Jamaicans,
in your Xaymaca, your land of wood and water
in your early Caribbean sun and sea and winds.
I take this coastal walk from Priestmans River
on to Long Bay and feel a place breath-soaked
and track-trampled by you, Arawak Indians
without donkeys or cattle or wheels or a gun.

Roofs cone-shaped, your round houses of straw
make a village, isolated or sprawling on,
drummed by rolling of the sea and sung to
by the squawks of macaws and parrots.
And in the chatter on the seasound light,
helper children too colour-streak the day
while nearly naked men dig into the bulk
of a fallen silk cotton tree with instruments
of stone, wood and bone to find
a canoe there in the trunk oversized.

At another house other men make traps for fish
as they could have been tricky crosses of wood
with a noose to hold wild hogs, iguanas, birds.
At another house, other men and women make
ornaments, cloths, hammocks, instruments.

Further away, bordered by flame trees, guava,
starapple – away from the ordered crops
of cassava, maize, arrowroot, sweet potatoes
and the bitter broad leaves of robust tobacco –
the backs bent as if on all-fours are women
sowing well soaked grain into fresh land.

And noises of excitement lead me. I stand
in a clearing of wood
seeing batos, your ball game, played.

On smooth stones arranged, spectators sit.
Centrally on carved stools
the caciques are together.
Eyes follow the ball, hit by shoulders or head
to receive explosions of praises
mixed with groans and wailful contempt.

And from tracks that lead me now, I see
at every house the manes of black hair dressed,
light brown skin specially painted. And a travel
of cooking and brewing embraces me: A festival!
The building up of a festival. That
collecting of extravagance.

And I stand where all happens – grand place
of that man who receives the best of sea
and land harvests, the only one who
when in the trauma of death will be
honour-strangled – grounds of the cacique's house.
From everywhere, one people have come.

Striped and painted flat in red,
yellow, black, many men are also
feather cloaked and feather head-dressed.

In sounds of leg rattlers and other shell
ornaments, in chants of cries and groans,
good spirits are honoured against bad ones.
In his painted and plumed glory, with pendants
and amulets and bone and shell adornments,
the cacique leads the parade around the village
beating a wooden gong. At the rear
priests follow singing songs
that their voices alone will not defile.
At the grounds of the cacique's house
it is the time for the feasting and drinking,
the wild singing and dancing, and smoking.

And like returning from fishing
your canoes come in from other places
and from other parts of your island.
Like birds know their flight tracks
you know your way on the sea.
Your song of prophecy tells
of behind-the-horizon strangers
who one day would arrive with bodies covered
and armed with a thunder and lightning.

Truly, one day, ploughing the high seas
with maps and guiding instruments
and a guessing eye on a star,
well heightened with dreams of gold

and spices and wealth and power,
Columbus and men arrived
on your island of Xaymaca.

You brought gifts to Columbus.
You sought exchanges.
You sought new knowing Columbus brought.
Was it true, a leader grasped
Columbus' sword and blooded himself?
Was it true you pondered
on these newcomers as gods?

Carrying a Spanish official across a river
you planned and dropped him in,
held him down
and saw him drown.
You stayed, you waited, watched
and saw he really rotted.

And in the new truly human tones and rhythms
you were made slaves
and victims of diseases you could not stop.
You were harassed and distressed.
You died everywhere,
You poisoned yourselves in groups
and hung yourselves in company.
You dressed up your families and drowned yourselves.
In the slow new years you quickly vanished.
Every one!

And as if you did not first fish
and swim in this sea and these rivers
and grow your food and tobacco on the lands,
and hear these birdsongs
falling in the faces of leaves, history dates
your existence by sailors' arrival.

I sit now on the edge of this cliff.
I look out and over sunlit waves, remembering
the sea as your farm and highway.
Remembering – your huddled bones in caves.
Like humans, like the sea, the land effaces.
My African footprints overlay yours.

Kitchen News

Punsie O Punsie
sunhot cook the backra
like boil lobsta.
Poor man come in half dead
like fry up in anatto red.

Punsie O Punsie
go see the cook-up face.
Go see poor backra state.

Go see if he can left so
or if we should go
and oil him down
or jus fan him and fan him down.

backra: a white person; *anatto*: a dark orange-red colouring from anatto berries
used in cooking.

Afternoon Sunhot

Watch palm trees they swing
blue sky red hibiscus
in strangle of twigs and vines

and the stream cool
hardly a-gargle
speckled sun buttons

and birds
never did care –
jus a-whistle
and sing

mongoose a-prowlin hard
a-look and shriek fo blood

My Arrival

Showing the creature I landed
I slipped from my mother's womb
flesh connected, laced in a blood-spatter.

My father waited with a bottle of rum.
The moon floated somewhere.
The sea drummed and drummed our coastline.
Mullets darted in wooded streams.

A good night to end labour – Saturday.
The country-midwife held me up,
'Look. Is yu third boy child!'
My mother asked, 'Him all right?'

'Yes – all eyes, all ears.
Yes – all hands, all feet.'
My mother whispered, 'Thank God.'
My granny said, 'My Jim-Jim.
My husband! You come back?'

I slept.
Roosters crowed
all around the village.

In the sun's hot eye
my umbilical cord was dressed
with wood ash, castor oil and nutmeg
and buried under a banana-sucker.
There, a tree made fruits, all mine.

Haiku Moments: 2

5

New baldheaded glow
again, skyline-face, you start
your old round of climb.

6

Cocks chase gathered hens
Village pigs all squeal for feed –
another sunrise,

7

Smells of brewed coffee,
sprats frying up, yams roasted –
soon, church bell for school.

8

Going, dog leads man,
man rides the donkey slowly
leading the white goat.

My Cousin Rosetta

The river washed her breasts,
trees dressed her with beads:
she sits encamped behind the hill.

In her hut, she looks in
the broken and speckled mirror
and sees her face
weather-worked, unrouged,
and hair tangled, fibre stubborn
like a pile of coconut coir.

Dismayed, she dreams of how
and how she might conform
with trends she sees in town.

She has tried.
The pink powder she patted on
mismatched the brown of ther face.

She sits down, discontent
with a body dawn-dusky, longing
to be styled on world highstreets
in all O all that is newest.

Early Days Thinking Is Only So Much

I didn't think I shouldn't be hungry
I didn't think of government
I didn't blame my father's husbandry
everything was just as it was

I didn't think a bellyful
of nothing was nothing
I didn't think I didn't deserve nothing
when there was food
there was everything
and there was a lot I knew

I knew we should bow
to the well-rounded people
bow to the best educated people
bow to the whitest faces
go to school breakfast or not
and that was just how it was
and that would have to be right

Our everyday business was havenots' business
and we worked and joked and played games
and laughed often as we could

And fruit-season or famine
or flood-time or drytime
everything was just as it was

And I didn't think that anything
was wrong or anything was right
that education and knowhow should be
a mystery like witchcraft

It was just as it was
and everything would have to be right

Bluefoot Traveller

Man
   who the hell is you?
What hole you drag from
   and follah railway line
   pass plenty settlement
   sleep under trees
   eat dry bread and water
   sweat like a carthorse
   to come and put body
   and bundle down in we village?
How we to feel you not obeah-man
   t'ief
   Judas with lice
   and a dirty mout?
Why you stop here? Get news
   Mericans open up dollar place
   in we districk?
Here we got woman givin away
   to follah-line man –
   and water an donkey and lan?
Bluefoot
   I considerin you hard hard
I point out to you –
   move!
It in my bones deep deep –
   pick up possessions
   walk again
An you don't call out
   a battalion of fists
   don't pull down
   hills of rockstone
   don't bring out
   woods of lickle bumpy sticks
   to drop on your head-top
   an crack it up.

obeah-man: witchcraft man.

Faces Around My Father

Hunger stormed my arrival.
I arrived needing.
I had need of older selves.
My mother's milk met
my parching. Streams were here
like stars and stones,
and a fatherhood compelling.

Fatherhood tailed a line
of fathers, we knew: a prehistory
book, a full season open all time,
a storehouse for emptying
for renewal, a marketing
of strength that stuffs away
richness of summers upon summers.

I'd work up a clean slate full.
Crafts and arts would engage me,
my urgent hands would grow
in homely voices,
the land would amaze
my roaming eyes,
incite my impulses.

Head striped, sir, with sounds
of birds in the hills,
sweat smells in clothes stuck
with soil and sun, you come
into the house at evening
like a piece of hillside.
I wait to take your drinking mug.

A silence surrounds your eating.
The dog catches and gulps
pieces of food you pitch
that somehow cut your distance.
A son washes your feet.
Another brings glowing firewood:
you light up your pipe.

Your incidental money getting
not believed, a child asks for cash
for boots or book.
Our words are stones
tossed on a genial guest.
You vanish into twilight.
A sleeping house receives you back.

And father is a scripture
lesson. Father knows
blueprints of seeds in the moon,
knows place of a cockerel's
testicles, knows coins
in minutes. His body sets
defences, sets boundaries.

Yet strong hints had soaked us:
we are not beautiful,
we are a cancellation
of abundance and sharing.
I am charged with unmanageable
hunger. I am trumpeted
for ungettable distances.

I must cross our moat of sea,
and I have no way. I must list
lost tracks, must write
my scanning of time, must plant
hot words in ministers like cool
communion bread. Yet I should drown
in language of our lanes.

In and about your preclusion, sir,
dead footsteps entrapped me.
You chopped wood and sang,
I listened behind a wall.
In hot field of pineapples
fermenting, I watched you
dreaming: I walked away.

Your tool's edge touched work
barely, and you resharpened.
Sir, in fresh sunny magnitude,
your dramatic grind of machete
should flatten forests. Yet
you left for work looking,
'What boss shall I serve today?'

Were you being your father
or just a loser's son? Sir,
did old scars warn vou to yield
and hide? Were you strangely
full of a friendly enemy
voice? Did you feel
your movements failure-fixed?

Schemed in your steady
good health, we were placed
to proliferate loneliness,
birthdays of lacks,
trouble growing in our flesh,
lips moved by ventriloquists,
beginnings with approaches of daggers.

We needed that safety, sir,
that wonderment of caressing eye,
that steadiness that allows
strongest and sweetest voice,
that sanctioned contentment
that walked bright
in the constellation of children.

Our voices deepened,
our limbs emulated trees,
our appetites expanded,
our silence encircled you
like strangers with killer plans.
I disowned you to come to know
thanks to connection that someone may feel.

I saw your body full
and fit and free, ready
in the sun's recycle,
ever the husbandman
of exalted acclamations.
I saw you die, sir,
well bluffed by subjugation.

Folk Proverbs Found Poems

1

Stump-a-foot man can't kick
with his good foot.

2

Tiger wants to eat a child, tiger says
he could swear it was a puss.

3

Is a blessing me come me see you:
eye-to-eye joy is a love.

4

Is better to walk for nothing
than sit down for so-so.

5

A man with half-a-foot
must dance near his door.

6

Good-friend you can't buy.
Cheap bargain takes money.

7

Better go heaven a pauper
than go hell a rector.

8

If ants waller too much in fat,
fat will drown ants.

9

Stretch your hand and give
it's a God own grace.

stump-a-foot: stumpy or one-legged.

In Our Year 1941 My Letter to You Mother Africa

I sit
under the mango tree in our yard.
A woman passes along the village road,
loaded like a donkey.
              I remember
I start my seventeenth year today
full of myself, but worried, and sad
remembering, you sold my ancestors
labelled, *not for human rights,*
And, O, your non-rights terms were
the fire of hell that stuck.
                    Mother Africa
my space walks your face
and I am condemned.
I refuse to grow up fixed here
going on with plantation lacks
and that lack of selfhood. Easily
I could grow up all drastic and extreme
and be wasted by law.
I want a university in me as I grow.

And now
three village men pass together,
each gripping his plantation machete.
              I remember
we are stuck in time and hidden.
I refuse to be stuck in a maze
gripping a plantation machete.
l refuse to be Estate 'chop-bush' man
and a poverty path scarecrow.
Refuse to live in the terror of floods
and drought, and live left-out and moneyless.
I refuse to worry-worry Jesus Christ
with tear-faced complaints. And, O, I refuse
to walk my father's deadness,
Schooled to be wasted lawfully
and refuse it
I am doubly doomed to be wasted by law,

                    Mother Africa
New World offices and yards of rejection
threaten me, like every shack dweller seared
by poverty and feels disgraced.
And people positioned to make changes
are not bothered how poverty sinks in.
Help stop my vexed feelings growing.
Help me have a university in me.

          And now
          a banana-truck passes.
                    I remember
I dread that cap-in-hand
my father. His selfhood gutted –
all seasoned plantation corned-pork –
no education habit is there.
Not seeing his need and his rights
to help make the world free,
not seeing the club of countries
that confiscated his ancestors' lives
still set his boundaries, not seeing
no god for our good with us,
my father demands no more
than a small cut of land, hidden.
                    Mother Africa
nobody at home here has any
education habit. Nobody stirs differently.
And I want life of the world in print.
I want to move about in all ages.
Not stay deformed, arrested, driven
by any drillmaster's voice telling
the growing good of myself is cancelled.
I want to be healed of smashed-up selfhood,
healed of the beating-up by bad-man history.
I want a university in me as a man.

          And now
          children pass by, going to loiter
          around the tourist beach.
                    I remember
you were pillaged easily
and gutted easily. Existing dumb

you lost your continental wealth,
our inheritance, my inheritance.
And, a settled absence, you are a fixed
nonparticipator I never see. And while
others come and go from their motherlands,
I live marooned, renamed 'Negro'
meaning, of no origin,
not eligible for human rights.
                    Mother Africa
I walk your face
and my heritage is pain.
And there somewhere
you make not one move.
Say nothing. Do nothing.
And I feel excessive doings could grip me.
I could call on bad doings as normal
and be wasted by law.
I want a university in me.

          And now
          at our gate, a village beggar stands
          calling my mother.
                    I remember
I am third generation since slavery,
born into people stricken in traps,
Eight generations departed
with a last sigh, aware they leave
offsprings all heirs to losses,
to nothing, to a shame, and to faces
who meet enmity in the offices
of their land and the world.
You say nothing, do nothing
while your bosom's gold and gems are stars
in other people's days
around the world. And scattered
stubbornly, we are here
in the sun's comings and goings
anguished for our human status back.
                    Mother Africa
do you know, cruelties of your lacks
join forces with New World mangling?
Now I want to be healed.
I want university.

And now
village voices go by
strong with the adjective 'black'
in their curses.
I remember
in lessons at school you were degraded.
No village man accepts his photographs
that printed him truly black.
You never made a contact
never inspired me
never nurtured, counselled or consoled me.
I have never seen you, Africa,
never seen your sights or heard your sounds,
never heard your voice at home,
never understood one common
family thing about you beneath
one crinkly head or naked breast.
Any wonder I have no love for you?
Any wonder everybody at school despised you?
Tradition has it, our people's travel
to you does not happen. Visits
to a motherland are overlords' privilege.
What is your privilege?
Mother Africa
I want university.
Is there any help in you?
Will I have to store,
or bag-up and walk with, inherited hurt
and outrage of enslavement?
Will I transcend it?
Or will I grow up wasted
in deformity or being outlaw?

TWO

Charged

Driven to bathe in the light
of scattered and deepest words
they arrive crazy for diamonds.
Backed by army and navy.

They face the others –
trap-injured lions.
An outpouring
of excuses.

Driven to have balm-oil baths
all meet. Armoured, armed with knives.
Impelled for kisses
they meet. Cloaked with abuses.

Come. Needing exchanges.
They make a Babel
on having most
and having best.

Driven to learn. They come.
They declare all-knowing.
Seeing they are humbled
all strike up noisiest fanfare.

New Catalyst Listening

Comes – opens our gate.
Comes – across our grass.
Parched and pinched.
Unripe – yet wrinkled like raisin
smelling of waste and weather
talking gibberish.
Comes and stands at our door.
Wants fruit of a private garden.

Comes – knocks our door.
Two-legged mudhole drinker.
Damned well bred on waste.
Bred on owning all that state –
that sameness of poverty.
Made in havenots' habits and looks.
Shaped in news that's damned bad news.
And – trampled down boundaries!

Comes and stands.
Nothing inheritor.
One pot minder.
Skills – the tying of sticks
with yearnings to pay bills.
Wants privilege earned.
Wants to have a castle cracked!

Lion

Body colour of hay, big cat.
Staring face a fearless look.
A superstar nature presents,
getting featured more
than eagles flying and whales swimming.

Hunger switches you on, big cat.
Padded toe-walk breaks
into trots, into athletic dash.
You flash claw-daggers and crusher-jaws
to hug a zebra
and kiss and cap the nose and mouth.
O what a love for flesh!
What a stunning show, devouring
someone different at only contact!

Vermin and flies choose you, big cat.
Night sky carries your quaking roars
in company with fellow lions only.

Your beauty, your strength, your success
fix you with a dread
of your devouring.
Do creatures like you ever feel
a hollow of helpless loneliness?

A Lion Electioneers

Lions lions welcome! welcome!
Your every vote is for 'well done'
keeping our sights
right on our pride and rights.

Fellow lions, we must settle
our totally safe tangles
with losers, and fix
our legal non-risk and social non-mix.

We vote to manage
and preserve our heritage
for our own little chubby cubbies –
not the little wasted waifies.

We vote for our purity,
our blest first quality,
never to be diluted
by others, lessers, and the corrupted.

Facing pressure to change,
facing that challenge,
we face a rebellion
by the lower millions.

Not to stop this rot,
set by that ugly lot,
we'll not diminish,
we'll slowly vanish.
Vote to be and be legal!
Vote to settle what is traditional!

In all your hundreds –
ROAR...!

You see, fellow lions,
mighty, mighty, fellow lions,
we inherit an open field,

inherit what it may yield,
to meet our special hunger –
we the powerful who command wonder.

Every bone new iron,
isn't every frame a lion?
Every sinew all passion,
isn't every move a lion?

Just as never any Hercules,
never any such Androcles.
Of all of the tribes –
only one unbroken pride in the prides.

In the blood, traditional,
as winners, we are natural.
In the service of being fed on,
lower things serve higher ones.

In all your hundreds –
ROAR…!
And ROAR…!

Separating off is natural.
We only want it legal.
Face truth
you see truth.
Face separate male
you see separate female.
Face separate tribes
you see the best in family prides!

With nothing of curses,
the pure live by victories.
With other systems for failures,
the cursed live by losses.

You stay the most complete
you see your natural meat
in the bodies of the weak
all as good steak.

You live skilled and strong with wits,
inferiors grow on your shit.
You make more and more successes,
inferiors make more asses.

Dilute who you are
you kill a star.
Mix your born worth
you walk a half a sloth.
Wake up with a warthog
you get trailed by little frogs.

Want to sing the blues –
start putting on shoes.
Want to start to coo –
go be a gobbler in a zoo.
Want no hot meal ready –
go push supermarket trolley.

Want to be in a circus –
be a clown being bogus.
Want a real tomorrow
then back a real Leo.

For, you want a bit
you swallow a rabbit.
You want everything
you stay king! And stay king!

In all your hundreds –
ROAR...!
And ROAR...!
And ROAR...!

Fellow lions fellow lions,
for simple continuation
we vote to stay undefiled –
stay pure, stay wild and wild!

No taking home
sorry tales and worms.
No burdened with louts,
half deads and down-and-outs.

No taking home losers
and taking home whingers.
No. Better a home of bones
than a home of stones.

Celebrate O celebrate
living separate,
not with anything of hate,
just with time-tested Apartheid,

Here under sky
in every eye
staying best, staying strong –
stay so, ever long.

The best evolved,
the best developed,
no further to go
and none else to say so –
only with our ways to be legal –
we say, we are THE FINAL!

Vote to preserve best head of the heads!
In all your hundreds –
ROAR...!
And ROAR...!
And ROAR...!
And ROAR...!

Riot

On and on in a night
of thudding and jawfuls of blood
and skin of gravel and glass,
flames flash and flash.

Quickly, bodies change places.
Groups of hands make
an earthquake, separately.

Street-lamps cry shattered cries.
Gutted shops are helpless
like cars turned over,
lamp-posts leaning down,
a building that explodes,
billboards that are scorched
and people who are smeared.
Littered streets are
stoned and trackless woods.

What is this?
An impulse of charged recklessness
or substitute movements for money spending?
An emptying of institutions' guts
or an outburst of locked-up skills?
Is it a street dance of pain?

Light lost, darkness returns.
You look on spellbound.
Free routines are cancelled.
Ripped and bruised, lawmen agitate.
Undamaged faces watch on, twisted.

Is this a release
of all offensives?
Or is this a mangling
only to show the power
of dead days evoked?

A Stopping of Time to Call

You have excited her now.
You started the flapping
of that abrasive wheel: heart
so tightly tied steadily,
a pain manufacture place.

You are still far, far, you know,
from a welcome in this house.
You watch madness. You see that
to occupy seventy stolen chairs
one wild fat woman on and on
bruises herself through nights.

But you are guilty of arousal.
You have knocked a door.
You have shaken a ghost to life.
You have brandished account demands,
impossible to settle straight.

What Is No Good?

I will stop
night's return,
stop dawn, stop dusk,
leave your eyes on
white dazzle of noon.

I will let sea rocks move
and fill in dark depths of oceans,
let storm clouds
and November be whitened,
leave you the glitter of space.

I will wash out
the brown of earth,
bleach out the tarmac of roads,
let gardens be white roses only,
leave you brilliant desert ways.

Sunlight's tanning
I will cancel,
leave you the show
of a tree
newly stripped of bark.

I will leave you time
with a dazzling face,
leave you a pale pale red
fixed on each other.
Would absence be abundance?

Summer in the Senses

1

I dreamed in waterfalls.
Music absorbed my evenings.

I ate I watched TV I read.
I jogged I sweated I washed I slept.

I stepped here I stepped there.
I found I swam I sunned myself.

I stared at exhibitions.
Shapes of strange opposites recurred on me.

Humming I stroked my cat close.
Reading I ignored my cat.

Sighing in summers
I searched faces.

I took in soft flowering of gardens.
Took in high ragged rocks aloof and austere.

I came to tunnels and was swallowed.
I brought stars close.

Now – incredible – since we found us
I see my search was how I waited

meeting areas of you in things –
areas of you in all the elements.

2

Getting immersed in you is relief
like reason disappears
in your voice and company
or thinking of you writing it down
or O when we hug
and I just fly to oblivion.

Since every act we do is really
for our locked away moments,
let's start a selfassertive club,
no – a holiday club, where
all the entertainment is
abandonment
which will keep us to rule number one –
that no member's allowed absence
because NAKED AND SHAMELESS CLUB has
a total membership of two –
me and you.

She thinks –
Wanting love he's rough,
getting it it's not enough
seized with a search in a place
like an ocean's depth.

He thinks –
Wanting love she's stormy,
getting it she's stormy
wanting to receive like earth taking rain.

She says –
The priest blessed my face:
it dressed me like a veil.
That's why I sleep heavenly
in one shadow we make
in movements or stillness.

She says –
The sun is out. I am out.
All around me I am out.
I must have a baby. If
I can't have your baby
my navel will sprout crocuses
and my ears cherryblossoms.
I'll gather my offsprings
I'll wrap them in a shawl
I'll give them to you,
staring, staring
with all of my silence.

Ol Style Freedom

Darlin mi darlin
you lying down
all legs belly bosom face
quiet-quiet in room here
All of all so much –
street poverty can't touch me now
Hurts – threats – banished away

No pockets on me
  I a millionaire
No test before me to fail me
  I know I know everything

Darlin mi darlin
you the offerin with all things
  all of all so much
every tick of clock stopped
every traffic groan switched off
every peep of bird shut up
only sea waves risin risin

Hope she fixed sheself fo no-baby
            fixed sheself fo no-baby
I in a king time king time king time
  king time
      king time
          king time...

Young Year Harassment

Busy gardens urgent again
the charged land arouses,
compels and unsteadies her.
At her window she endures
the land's fresh colours like pain.

And the sun's new echoing aches.
It grasps deeply and stirs
hopes she cannot go after.
It harasses a deformed frame
like a seed entered to be popped.

That sun was wild. That sun was
a rustic costumed reveller
who would drag her off to Carnival
not seeing any attempt would be
only a stagger and a fall.

Taken outside and left
she gropes
on the hillside on her knees
clawing at elusive strands
she feels there in her hair, somewhere.

All so heightened and pressing
the sun's walk brings demands
like unmanageable foreplay.

She pulls and pulls her blouse open.
Wind kisses her sigh after sigh.
Grass folds away teardrops.

Phantom Loving

In the red-light circle
in the darkened room,
the woman on the floor
stripteases mirror-framed
down to the drama of nakedness.

An inward self desired out,
in different taboo ways
in the pangs of delicate sounds,
she caresses herself open.

Her smile an innocent
garden-size red rose,
her flesh surrenders
heights of pleasure peaks.

Exposure absorbs her:
the men are silent, centred, lost.

The finely suited among greasy jeans,
the stick aided among sound limbs,
the manicured hands among dirt-stained,
all are religiously engrossed

like the thousands who file in
and out, who stand and sit focussed
on a woman in the fire of love
aching in pretence, for them.
And they go silently.

Accomplice

Like emotions lit by gold
flesh eating is a loving
the lover shows a claim to
that the loved also enticed.

Open eyes are nets
like sharp experts ready
with precise inbuilt gauge
for a swift sizing up.

And who won't persuade
or straightly crack
mind or matter open
to have the ostentation?

Yet who is a victim
and is not in
as contributor to it?

Probing

I probe long into deep-deep night.
Woods let go leaves willingly.
Rage for summers past is trapped
down under sleeping lids.

Hoardings and skeletons live together.
Proprietors and hungry eyes
crisscross unnoticeably.

Celebrated hands polish walls
loved excluders, golden.

I search workings of night.
Darkness seethes with new awakenings.
A new day awakens
not only by window light.

I Am on Trial After Being Juror on a Black Man

Fear, don't trouble me, don't
drag me down. I'll look around
this court and not surrender.
I mus burst up the bite
of knife-edge words.
I mus fence miself with fists.

All the same another
doomsday. Another time
of trapped feet walled up.

Another lot of captors.
Robots encircle me
with power of law
in priest robes,
in robes of angels
and the uniform
of the blue clothes gang.

Man, take it. Take it
man! At sweetest we attack.
We get each other or plan
it. And I am caught,
noosed, because I survive; .
because I move where I belong
and dance my survival.

Always my backing is weak.
But I won't break up, before
eyes of knowhow
as my people always fall,
sharing majesty of a room
watching swirls of robes,
victims in a classic show.

I wasn't born to satisfy
the skills of robots.
I wasn't born to be bullseye.

I was born because
I was born
like tree and bird and star.
Tomorrow, I must get away.

A man must feel his woman's leg.
A man mustn't fight,
fight, fight between trees,
between walls
between lamposts
to have a sightless moment
overshadow him like a net.

I wasn't born to be turned
into outlaw. I was
born like everyone,
with different fingerprints
and a different face
and have to find my way
through everybody.
And I have to find my way.

I look at the jury.
See me push back a giggle,
for jackass,
their little black juror:
man drilled to kill he smile.

See the robots whisper,
like lovebirds, for me
to see them as gods.
And let them toss about
questions about me. Let them
play ping-pong with my life
and movements.

They can never know
I can't agree. I can't agree
I was born a failure. I can't
agree I was born disqualified.

I can't agree I was born
the material for robots to pulp
into their successes.

They can never know I was born
because a man must
fight back, and not
accept the role of dirt.
Them wi neva see I mus add-to
an add-to all mi weakness them
or find strength of a storm.

Hitting back keeps everybody
absorbed, keeps me
with a big backlog
of moves to make up.

And they will hurt me well.
And they will know they please
everybody. And they will watch
to see if I rise. And I
will rise, at hours and places
in unexpected ways.

And my face changes
as I've never known it.
And I don't laugh, over
the people I make mourn,
and make me mourn, like my
accomplices here in robes.

And they dangle me
on rope-ends of words.
They focus robot faces
on me, like a squad of gunmen.
They toy with my life.

And no more an apology
I can't hide my eyes.
No more a repentant rubbish
a man must eat and wear
and drink and dance.

A man must show:
I made it
I take
I win
I have. I have!
And they'll hide him away
as a maniac, knowing they have
all the holy, legal, regal connections.

And I unfocus my eyes.
My answers are merely
No and Yes.

And I remember. I remember,
the blue clothes gang came at me:
  How many white women you fucked?
  How many how many how many?
  How old how middle-aged how young?

I give no answer. Because
I give no answer, I get a blow
for every white woman I bedded,
they said, and every one
I wished to bed. I cried out
cried out cried out and said:
  Black women are not mine.
  Black women are not mine to keep.
  Can't you make friends?
  Is that why you punish me?

I am the object of the smokescreen
ceremony. I must speak
when spoken to. My answers
again are No and Yes.

The switches of robots spark
each other. I'm worthless, they say.
Everything I have is worthless.
I should be dumped
away from people
away from animals
away from God.

Yet when I stood here
for suspicious loitering
was it for that?
When I stood here
for removing goods
was it for that?
When I stood here
for stripping old people of money
was it for that?
When I stood here
for wounding, as I stand
here now, wasn't I wounded?

THREE

Thoughts Going Home

Twelve years of darkness and sea
between me and the village house
I ventured from, so far.

What lifetime hopes go back
with me? What disappointments?
What discoveries from eye to eye?

And seeing is now your fingers' edge
on shapes. And sounds defined keenly.
I will be a voice. Your son –
strange words with foreign airs.
And a full body – a change
from scarce and slender times.

How are you without sturdy legs
that firmly took sharp sunny hills
and wielded hoe, machete, axe,
and carried baskets of yams,
carried bundles of wood, across
muddy tracks and the rough lowlands?

How are you with slow searching
feet and empty eyes? How is it
alone, in a cave of night
continuously? Are we little ones
who engage you or lost men
whose return you await?

So much awakening never touched you.
But, mother, I have seen best educated
men, centrally celebrated men,
whose words to me showed their eyes
to be a day-old kitten.

A bright moon, it will be.
Shadows unknown sitting about.
Dim lamps on bare shelves.
Everybody asleep, guarded by uprights.

Will father glide in tonight?
Through the plain walls of cedar
he so loved? Or be a swift man-size
feather, down the rafter-ceiling?

Will I know the hibiscus road?
With my broken steps, will I find
the cottage that cradles home
with the old one waiting?

A Schooled Fatherhood

There in my small-boy years that day
couldn't believe the shock,.
the blow that undid me, seeing him abused,
reduced, suddenly. Helpless, without honour
without respect, he stood indistinct,
called 'boy' by the white child
in the parents' look-away, 'don't-care' faces.
Lost, in a peculiar smile – being
an error, a denial of the man I copied,
that big-big man I'm one day to be – he made
a black history I didn't know swamp me,
hurt me, terror-hands of a dreaded ghost.

Two men apart, from now – with him
not able to see, not able
to keep pace with time or know
my secret eye watchful –
I began to see
educated voices charging his guts
like invisible pellets of a gun
imbedding *in him*, daytime, nighttime.
And soon, he clean forgot
who he was. Then with his roots
and person's rights wiped away
he knew he'd known nothing always,
His deep man-structure dismantled,
a tamed dog came in him and gave him face
gave him readiness for his job –
delivering shot birds between his teeth
to get a patting beside high boots –
   my father
      my first lord
         my inviolable king.

Countryman O

Countryman O
wha happn then wha happn?

Me come a Kingston town
to look aroun
to look aroun me spend
mi only pound.

Countryman O
wha happn then wha happn?

Me come a Kingston town
to buy a yard a cloth
to buy a yard a cloth
me find mi money short,
Me find me buy one rum
and all money drink down.

Countryman O
wha happn then wha happn?

Friend and me had a row.
Meet up with him jus now
and say, 'Off you knees
with you *sorry* and *please*.
Like a decent bar bum
always the best of chum,
jus say to the barman:
'Give you friend halfbottle a rum.'

Countryman O
wha happn then wha happn?

Back Home Weddn Speech

Man-eye go and fall on woman
man-skin catch a-fire.
Woman say, 'Is me – why you on fire.'

Woman-eye go and fall on man
woman-skin flutter like storm.
Man say, 'Is me – why you born.'

Man-dread say, 'Oh! I gone and get
long belly horse
and must feed it like a good-cause!'
Woman say, 'Little calf in pasture
could turn out a bull-mother.'

Man-dread say, 'when money done
woman love done !'
Woman say 'Just like a good rum
woman go with a good man.'

Man-dread say, 'Marriage got teeth!'
Woman say, 'Marriage is *sweet sweet*,'

So, man and woman come
hold hands and say,
'The two of we so full of love
the two of we jus *have* to love.'

Haiku Moments: 3

9

Your spinning days worked
generations without pay –
O windmill here, dead!

10

Falling leaf scares him
yet out he strolls under trees –
does autumn test him?

11

With all of the storm –
thunder, winds, floods – whole rock sits
there loving the ground,

12

Forgetting the pains
of childbirth again she's there
and now the birth-yell!

13

Water cut, lights fail,
now making little love, look
she gone dead asleep.

14

Miss Kate's water pan
not on head: in hand is fan
and hymnbook to church.

15

Nine-Night singing sad,
merry, nonstop – an owl hoots
in the one silence.

16

Thief thief mi one-goat,
hog-sick kill mi sow, Jesas,
now mi plantain cut!

17

Sun-hot sun-hot why
you wahn black-man sweat so like
him drink river up?

18

Her hands like a child's
work her flute sonata voice
and pull out my tooth.

Meeting Mr Cargill on My Village Road

Down from his donkey letting it
freely crop roadside weeds,
he shakes my hand grandly warm.
'Bless mi eye them now,' he says,
'Cousin Olmassa son, yu home.
Home from Englan! And fine fine
yu look. Like Christmas come
home-boy, whey yu stan up!

'And now, the world have
no father fo you.
Come home to find we bury him,
yu Olmassa, under yu mango tree.'

'I shave yu sleepin ol man.
I help bathe him,
give him he *last last* wash.
We dress him,
put him in he blacksuit and tie.
We lay him out, lay him out
in he own cedar board box, shinin.'

'Graveside bring everybody,
in full heart, full voice,
a-let him go in prayers and hymns,
a-give him he sixfoot down
and show a deserving traveller gone
to rest all him eighty-odd year.'

'And Nine-Night pass, at yu house.
Home yu didn come. But all,
everything, everything, happen
like yu was here, here on spot.'

Next time in my home village,
I didn't see Mr Cargill.
I saw only the new mound of earth
his own coffin replaced.

Starapple Time Starapple Trees

All around flame-trees blaze
a red acreage of domed tops.
Mouths are sweet stained.

Everybody eats the starapple.
Brown or purple or white
succulent ready flesh exposes
hidden star to open faces
of starapple time,

Enticing to be opened in
group-loving starapple time,
lips-luring round fruits grew
between limbs, growing
shadowed to readiness
near big boat cotton-tree erect,
washed by burning sun.

And apple-honey squeezed and sucked –
all else gone suspended –
who won't make joy noises
under canopy of coppery silk,
bridal in sunlight? Even
a woodpecker, in its dipping
flight, screams with laughter.

A Walk Through Kingston, Jamaica

My peripheral eye caught
familiar angles. I knew he hid
with the waiting people
of the city's backland.

My steps halted,
in joy in fear,
beside a bowed wreck.

It was a busily suspicious face,
something seldom aroused,
the clothes a stink nest.
My memory sharpened the jolly
stutterer at school.

My anxious voice bounced loose
like an old embrace of boyhood.
Leo, man! I said.

A glare unlidded his old
froggy eyes. A rush of memory opened
his mouth and arms. A twist
hardened a contemptuous mouth
in a knotted beard.

He slowly drew a final door.
It seemed my voice,
my dress, my look, wounded him
as if I was a foreign reporter,
to expose him, to say
he chickened out on his children.

His word staggering manhood
had linked his first girl, I knew.
He had sustained a fluency
of eight new lives. I knew
he had left them, years now.

But I knew him before all that.
Leo! My voice pulled
at his hurried and ragged turn away.
My early village friend was armless
and wordless for me.

Was this the final man?
There was no joke,
no touch.

Leo! I whispered.
His shuffles mounted
a wider and wider distance.

Defendant in a Jamaican Court

Yes I did chop him, sar.
I chop him.
I woz full-full
of the vexation of spirit, sar.

I woz beyon all ow I know me, sar –
over the odda side cut off
from all mi goodness
and I couldn steady mi han firm, sar.

I chop him shoulder.
I let mi distric man blood stream down.

Him did storm up mi bad-bad waters
that I couldn settle –
that flood me, sar –
that mek one quick-quick terrible shut-eye
when all mi badness did rule.

Words of a Jamaican Laas Moment Them

When I dead
mek rain fall.
Mek the air wash.
Mek the lan wash good-good.
Mek dry course them run, and run.

As laas breath gone
mek rain burst –
hilltop them work
waterfall, and all
the gully them gargle fresh.

Mek breadfruit limb them drip,
mango limb them drip. Cow, hog, fowl
stan still, in the burst of clouds.
Poinciana bloom them soak off, clean-clean.
Grass go unda water.

Instant I gone
mek all the Island wash – wash away
the mess of my shortcomings –
all the brok-up things I did start.
Mi doings did fall short too much.
Mi ways did hurt mi wife too oftn.

Worse Than Poor

Lord poor man poor
   him worse than poor
him is real miser
   and none the wiser

Him av one coin
   him wash the coin
and to av some silver
   him drink the water

Villager's Independence: 1

Every meal-time going be a meal-time.
Every child body going have clothes.
Every child going go school everyday.
Instead of a hurricane mash-up
it going be a hurricane of build-up.
And every house stan up to breeze-blow.

We going have a tractor to farm we land.
Woman head burden of load going to go
all along on four-wheel.
Rain-season rain not going sink. A new
reservoir going keep rainfall fo dry-time.
We going build up a real market.

Foot-track them going broaden out
into crossroad after crossroad them.
Big Pasture will turn new house settlement.
Aeroplane going come land in Bottom Wood
clearance. Ship across the world going stop
right here outside we Long Bay Beach.

Water like power going come live in
we house – a suitable quiet partner
always there with lectric light.
And when Queen-of-Englan come,
we going house her and home her
right here in we district.

Drum soun come and come through Island now
drummin hell spirit out everybody
and everything. Not to turn back.
It here. Not ever to go away.
Me hearing it good-good. All the new
new soun of mento full up me head.

Before God and before man
a change a-come.
It a-come.
Overdue, overdue, in we life!
Before God and before man
Independence a-come!

Villager's Independence: 2

Me not a poor man. Not a poor man.
Me dohn beg. Not lazy. Not sick.
Me have good houseful a children.
It only that mi boots in pieces
and me get swamp-over,
turn in a wretch *bad bad*,
with piece a rundown land
with dry-time, no donkey, no milking cow.

But, me not a poor man. Not a poor man.
Me a healthy man in charge
a mi little house, mi family, mi taxes.
It only that mi shirt is patchwork
on patch on mi back
and me get swamp-over,
turn in a wretch *bad bad*,
in a wet house with roof not get repair
and too much night-time bellyache groaning.

But, me not a poor man. Not a poor man.
Me a fit man. Rich in heart
and body and mind. Full a desire.
It only that mi mouth mash up.
Teeth them drop out and gone.
And me get swamp-over,
turn in a wretch *bad bad*,
with too much bony people them
touching me and crowding me
with bad-talk wrong-word them
what come back and come back and settle
every night in we house.

But when Jesus did say: the poor
you have with you always,
him didn mean me at all!
Me not a Poor man! Never was.
And Independence a-come to prove that!

City Church Prayer Meeting

A God-calling spell in every word,
Miss Katy prayed on, prayed on,
for mothers exiled in the world –
houseful of children fatherless,
houseful of children penniless.
Nothing to hold on to. Nothing.
Nothing to hold on to. Nothing.
Emptiness. Emptiness. Emptiness.

A God-calling spell in every word,
full meeting of women prayed on, prayed on.
Help Lord! Help Lord! Amen echoed.
Houseful of children fatherless.
Houseful of children penniless.
Nothing to hold on to. Nothing.
Emptiness! In a full world.
Emptiness. Emptiness. Emptiness.

Sounds of a Dreamer

(Remembering Bob Marley)

1ST VOICE:

    Two-blood passion man,
    come walk on.
    Come walk on and make the scene
    with usual incantatory spell.
    Come word-out a continued cry.
    Word out hell hauntings all *sweet sweet*
    Make bad-man history get a trial.
    Make rhythms echo death of pain,
    music tickle feet,
    load fall away.
    Come, man. Come walk on and make the scene.

2ND VOICE:

    Out on a limb, a cooing dove:
    could we love and be loved?
    Could we touch I and I to find
    wonders of eye to eye confined
    in a wash of redemption song.

1ST VOICE:

        O you spinner of storm into song
        like instrument of steel pan!

    Well well distressed
    he met the losers poverty dressed.
    Met them telling him:
    all through every night long
    all through every day long
    living stops the same –
    Bad-Dice Man beats them at the game.

2ND VOICE:

    Hungrybelly and Fullbelly dohn walk same track.
    And Hope was born affected.
    She was born crippled.
    And *such such* a good looker.
    Such fine dresser and responsive singer.

Hears music, hears paradise:
everything, everything, in her eyes.
Sings, you hear a reggae queen.
Loved by all each time seen.
Now just a haunting
of love that stresses hunger,
of love that stresses hunger.

But beaten down fire what a-smoulder
brings out yard of brothers and sisters
to a hymnal of the flaming reggae
in the music of roots what deh yah
a-keep the temple open for Jah.

1ST VOICE:

O you voice of sun-sounds
in peace-and-love globe rounds!

Well well distressed
he met the losers poverty dressed.
Met them telling him:
ways of an eternal job
keep up other sides wrong sides,
Making a good chance a game unfair.
Bad-Dice Man throws bad dice,
Bad dice, dice loaded. Loaded.

2ND VOICE:

Hungrybelly and Fullbelly dohn walk same track.
And the dream was affected.
She was born crippled,
yet helped his lyrics, and moves
that urged his peace and love
where too many two-sides are wrong sides.

But beaten down fire what a-smoulder
brings out yard of brothers and sisters
for the come in of calm time
in the come in of the holy wine
bringing in the hidden for discovery.

1ST VOICE:

O you fanfare echoing dayclean –
fresh echoes we ride on!

Well well distressed
he met the losers poverty dressed.
Met them telling him:
all through every night long
all through every day long
we the losers the generations left,
we still stand out here bereft.
Bad-Dice Man throws bad dice,
bad dice, dice loaded. Loaded.

2ND VOICE:

Trees a-blossom
but too much young fruits fall
like it was a custom.
Trees a-blossom
but too much young fruits fall
like it was a custom.
And the exodus, exodus, exodus
is O such a silent exodus!

All of you famine skeletons,
all of you moneyless daughters and sons,
say: brother, dohn cry.
Say: sister, dohn cry.
We are recollecting to collect back,
a-try for pace and space unplaced
for free rightness of a future,
for free rightness of a future.
The sea does not divide for us to cross
we have to swim and cut our path
And everything's gonna be all right.

1ST VOICE:

O, remember –
he walked town streets, all trendy
looking for a scene-change that's friendly
together head to head with Jah
a-confirm rights of person to person law.

Remember – sounds in the yard
from country horns and strings he heard
in the evening cleared of storm
when friends roasted up *fresh fresh* corn
and they walked in the love of others,
love recharging survivors,
in a little time
that was only such a little time.

2ND VOICE:

Wild love stands to devour;
tamed love will lend and borrow.
Losers survive with songs of stress;
winners live with excess.

Could we love and be loved
forever loving Jah
saying, say:
forever loving Jah,
forever loving Jah?

1ST VOICE:

O – you new bridge we use now
with a garland of gold on show!

I and I: expression for Rastafarian principle of unity between self
and self and self and another; *deh-deh*: is there; *deh yah:* is here.

FOUR

Demands of Freedom

(remembering Zimbabwe, 1978)

Today we meet hatred left
as unlidded heads.
My children tremble seeing
well kept hands are scalping knives.

Bland voices are dynamites in our shacks.
I feel unbodied needing
a garment to wrap in.

And soldiers go making patchwork holes
of beasts and fields.
And laughter is away like an alien breeze
distant in trellised wisteria.

Lament-singing, even, is absent.
Blood goes cold netting dust.
My sense of being human dismissed
I do not know if I exist.

Bushman Cousin

His reverberations
waken and redefine me.

A total diaspora man now
I am back with the flock,
bent on everything.

And, bushman, you in me
shot me like hell.

You are the mirror I look in now.
Whatever I put on turns to rags.
And starvation is out in my eyes.
I hear my voice echoing
death shaken up.

On city streets I walk
I look on like a hill beast.
The cock has crowed, denial over,
but it is a resurrection
without a heaven.

We – same man now. I am haunted.
more than when we gave songs in chains.
More than when the winds whispered
we are free! free! free!
and we took to valleys and hills
for leaves and roots.

You clamour hard in me to claim
myself and yourself that I scorned.
Hunger has us ablaze
for more than the land's offerings.
We are cracked clods in drought
for more than just water.

You are the mirror I look in now.
You let go voices in me like hounds.
You torment the loathsome brutes –
us in me – hopeless, before Mandela,
in that long night that would not move.

Old Man in New Country

I am both Watutsi and Pygmy.
I have shone the moment's glory.
I have been the total loss.

Both leaf and flesh grinder,
both sucker of milk and narcotics,
I have been full and still;
my knees have rattled without flesh.

My shoulder supporting spear and bag,
I have ambled along tracks,
shoeless and not clothed. With leaves,
with secret eyes, with butterflies,
I have been the sun's painting exhibited.

Needing not one machine,
no sounds marked down,
I grew certain with my skills.
From all streams
the seasons wake in my blood.

But challenges and attacks
have entangled my peace.
My bag has repeated emptiness
to my bed. My hands have attended wounds
of wars undeclared.

Now my world is new
I cannot find a waterhole.

Returning Returning

Sun returns and returns –
its vulture eye had seen
the many many mangled bodies fly-covered

the many many quiet enclosures
of weaponry, restocked,
the many many fields of heads

amassed for death,
the many many uniformed men
marshalled with guns.

And night too returns, endlessly.
On and on night returns.
Does night try to release
a magical shadow-touch in sleep?

Woman at Waterhole

Lord
we waterhole –
we well –
we waterhole dry.
It dry up.

Breeze-blow flattn we house
and mud-up we things
like before
and before.
Flood kill off we crop them
and make the children moan
like before
and before.

Now waterhole dry.
We well –
we waterhole dry up.

Who goin stop sky-fire
roast-up of we?
Who go save we one-cow
and one-pig and one-goat?
Who goin save the children them, O?

Lord
waterhole dry up.
We well –
we waterhole dry.
O – it dry up.

Peacefulness of Starving

Old sacks of sticks, clustered, uncomfortable
with desires, distant desires to move: young man
you and your people are a field of exhibits.
Light unwanted, eyes are sad and unphased.
Flies trample family faces. Acquiescence
tells disconnection is a reversal;
a ticking breaks up blood and muscle;
inner wings and wheels are jammed.
There was nothing. There *is* nothing.
Hopelessly nothing.
Melting flesh entangles breath.
No child comes home from school.
Nothing is west, north, south or east,
Every leaf is dust, every source
of milk and meat and grain.
Time places; time reverses; time deals with nothings.
Time takes over disconnections.
    O build conections. Build connections.
    Get greatest masters of music
    playing best symphonies for all madhouses.

No quarrels of hope for a new love:
hands are emptied of a taking, a giving,
a grasp, a thrust, young man.
Voice a song-forgotten bird.
Thoughts dead leaves down a misty shaft.
Body melts in self-bereavement.
A vague lust-reminder lifts your loins.
You did not eat. You do not eat,
My tongue rots goat's dung.
Nothing is west, north, south or east,
All water has sunk irretrievably.
Time places; time reverses; time deals with nothings.
Time takes over disconnections.
    O build connections. Build connections.
    Get prisoners to live communions with priests.

No impulses of a first love excite.
A broken food-web evidenced chasms.
Reversed for ploughing under,
phased out of seasons, out of contexts,
your fleshy ghosts sit under the hammer of minutes.
My thoughts dawdle on disjointed bones.
Nothing is west, north, south or east.
Time places; time reverses; time deals with nothings.
Time takes over disconnections.
    O build connections. Build connections.
    Dress up poverty-stricken people
    in richest, finest clothes:
    put them sitting, filling all seats of banquets.

Think up a Leader

Listen.
Hear him announced.
'Here he is –
knower of track to every fireside
sound sleeper on bare boards
good company on parched corn and water for dinner
the bringer
of new dimensions
new textures before the eyes
and bodies growing scarless
our sage
who brightens blackness
our floods on dry time
our builder after hurricane
our own man who talks "roots talk"
as well as "professor talk"
who finds the lost
who wakens the dead and all beginners
who is hard transparent glass
with deep reds and blues
our leader
here he is here he is
our man with eyes all round the head.'

Love Charm

Long fingernails clean.
Witchcraft man wears three snake-shaped
silver rings on each hand.
He smells of ganja, aromatic oils, rum.
He sits in a shadow tied to 7 hours drumming.
And in a figure of 8, in the earth like a snake,
he puts in washed curses of moon-talk bounced back,
puts in charm owner's name in the circle of the moon,
puts in egg broken in water on Easter Day and sun-warmed
then, the sign of a crossroad,
sun-dazzle of middleday poured from a calico bag,
darkness of middlenight poured from a calico bag,
3 drops of innocent tears from 3 virgin girls,
3 teeth of a lion,
the growing drive of 3 fields poured from a bag,
a bagful of inertness from towering rocks,
3 under feathers from a white rooster's wing,
pounded leaf-of-life, barks, and bitter weeds,
puts in a bagful of dryness from fresh wool,
a bagful of water wetness,
3 bagfuls of sea-wind salt,
a bagful of dead silence,
powdered blood from 3 ram-goat's head,
7 drops of dew.
He mixes all this. He mixes
in drumming and movements
of 7 faceless dancers passing 7 times.
He rolls it round in his palm.
He half flattens it.
He sews up his magic mix
in new leather, smelling.
And concealed, strapped to an arm
it hides like a clinging frog.

Happy Goodbye Song

You staring summer days and shut-eye nights
on beaten place and dried-up tenants
all people awaiting no-help

eye of burner sun
watcher of gunshots outflying stones,
impartial colluder –
   with your silent walk banish pain

You burner sun you wrinkler
gripping me into a goner
having me rotting under dazzle

watching me nakedly pocketless
watching me wretchedly moneyless
watching non-weapon loser
   with your silent walk banish pain

Now you hangers-on old ways –
invasion of pain desires
people-devouring fires
lacks in varied uniform

rage of need lashing
bodies tasselled crying
all brains blunted –
   wave goodbye
     saying you're spent

No you hangers-on old ways –
hidden jaws of hunger
eaters of victims beyond wonder
feeder on girls and boys out of life

glass-walled abundance taunting my worth
drills that have me establish what I loath
all bad news no-answers all-mystery –
   wave goodbye
     saying you're spent

You disordered force of the dipossessed –
the convenience for death and stress –
losers who fight generations later
   come equal now
      saying hello hello hello

Artist Mother at Nation House, Jamaica

(for Edna Manley 1900–1987)

Beneath deep Middle Passage tides
our early arts drowned.
Sugar claimed creative work.
But come on darkness and sunhot –
England and Africa-touch empower her.
Quick-eye releases her
O so well.

In the drives of a new sun
she arrives. She sees
a static time.
Drought ongoing.
Yet pool settles –
bottomless, complete, secure.

Free and fine and fresh
a facility washes history
pain from faces.

The deepening bright hands
caress vision –
sketching, moulding, carving
to find emotion bodied
in mahogany like redwood shapes
angled with struggle
and triumph, defiance and hope.

Again and again strong strong she rises
holding another sacred sign,
another family member
positioned with all impulse to fly –

NEGRO AROUSED / MARKET WOMEN / TOMORROW /
HORSE OF THE MORNING / THE ANGEL /
PAUL BOGLE / JOURNEY...

Hills come down lower.
People move up taller.

Come on then darkness and sunhot.
Come on hungrybelly to strip us –
morning not morning to get lost with us.

At spacious work realm
she nurtured new days –
a source that stayed
not far from onehundred years.

Walk good. O walk good
like eye of a rising day
rolling out over land and over sea.

Fast Bowler

Batman's nervous wait – not a bowler's worry.
Upright wickets taunt him.
Back turned. He walks on.
A journey, long, long and steep.
Eleven men toss one ball with his arm.
Yet, ball speaks *his* eloquence.
He turns. He trots. He runs. Big long limbs
fly with pounding hoofs to a leap,
releasing a bullet of a ball.
Batsman ducks. Shelters in lower air.
Okay. Okay. Next time.

Back turned. Slowly, he walks, journeying.
Each wicket stands there – an enemy soldier.
That bat on guard. A fortress door.
Ball in hand is his charge
to despatch a man.
Ball stamps the pages of a life.
He turns. He trots, He runs. Big long limbs
fly with pounding hoofs to a leap,
releasing a bullet of a ball.
Batsman pad up. Two columns of pads.
Okay. Okay. Next time!

Back turned. Slowly, he walks, journeying.
Ball in hand is a nation's voice.
Jibes of standing wickets bite him.
Ball – *be* hurricane-powered!
He turns. He trots. He runs. Big long limbs
fly with pounding hoofs to a leap,
releasing a bullet of a ball.
Batsman hits him. Hit his ball away for four.
Loose ball. Avoid that. Avoid that.

Back turned. Slowly, he walks, journeying.
Ball tests hard how two nations can rub.
Sometimes with a spear disguised, sometimes
with a sword, gaming in an open field is
a battle, but *open*. And eyes watch him while
so erect, lordly wickets mock him.

Improvised ball, go now, arrive unreadable.
A baffler with the tricks of a genius.
He turns. He trots. He runs. Big long limbs
fly with pounding hoofs to a leap,
releasing a bullet of a ball.
Batsman hits him. Hits his ball away for six.
Unbelievable. Unbelievable. Think. Think!

Back turned. Slowly, he walks, journeying.
Wickets together. An immovable barrier.
Ball unravels an opening by combat.
Ball demands a total testing.
Eyes of his team rest on him heavily.
He turns. He trots. He runs. Big long limbs
fly with pounding hoofs to a leap,
releasing a bullet of a ball.
He misses the wickets by a pinpoint.
His missile! *His* missile! Controlled!
Launch it. Launch it, again, Launch it!

Back turned. Slowly, he walks, journeying.
Fine clothes get full of a downpour:
his fit limbs are heavy with fatigue.
But his arm works his nation's arm!
So knock him for ones and knock him for twos.
Have him glided to the boundary
or fly gone past the keeper. Have him
give a wide, a no-ball, a catch dropped,
and a spell without a wicket, and remember,
always, his next ball will carry his plan.
He turns. He trots. He runs. Big long limbs
fly with pounding hoofs to a leap,
releasing a bullet of a ball,
shattering the wickets to scattered sticks.
Got him! Got him! Let him walk.
O let him walk away, dead!

Shifting Boundaries

Clouds broke up, vanished, reappeared.
Ideas grew from strawbeds
to featherbeds, for waterbeds.
By habit, by dread of barriers,
I did not plan a move or a change.

Sea-waves emptied in sand, on and on,
Boats moved in and out of seaports.
Land-ports came in for aeroplanes.
And sour with ancestors' agonies,
dreading the dreads other faces kept,
my parents planned no changes.

Wheels rolled round and round the globe.
And, to get the moon footprinted,
generations of geniuses tested jobs.
I did not plan a move, and no
persons or authority planned it.
Then old pains in Europe exploded
the blood of its tribes.
Oceans divided for a pathway:
my isolation was gone.

Excluded from change, I find
I have broken free from encampments
behind hills, into a puzzling
vision and a noisy voice.

My change not planned, I find
I mix consciousness now knowing
I am right who and where I am.
My going unmask faces. And when
judgements on me suspend ideals,
old certainties become questionmarks.
Yet, I sleep, I wake, alarmed
feeling, no child overcrowds the world;
no land is resourceless.

Masked People, One People

Is we in a tinkle-jangle of bells and beads –
we – who play more than man-and-woman breed
in artworks
at footworks
in limbs a-rage
in rhythm rampage.
    Is everybody the carnival.

We group up CRESCENT-AND-STAR.
We group up PATCHWORK PAUPERS.
Is you and me GREAT QUEENS AND KINGS.
Is we turn GOLDEN WINGED-THINGS.
We group up LEO
and group up VIRGO.
We group up POCO PEOPLE
and BALMYARD PEOPLE.
    Is everybody the carnival.

Is you and me with chants
dispelling wants.
Is we like caged birds flown
in sharp whistles blown,
wild in sunshine on and on
in drums and beat of pan
with spears pointed up
and flags that flap.
    Is everybody the carnival.

We group up MASAI WARRIORS
and ABORIGINE RAIN DANCERS.
We group up DEVILS AND PRIESTS
and BUDDHA'S FOOTPRINTS.
We group up FERTILTY GODDESSES
and RELEVANCE OF SNAKES.
Look how he's ALL HAIR OUT OF A CAVE
and she TWO LOCKED HEARTS OF LOVE.
    Is everybody the carnival.

Look how she is BAD BABYLON WITH GUNS
and he DRAGON
and he CHIEF OF AMERICAN INDIAN
stuck in a dance delirium.
Is we the silver trees of COURTING MACAWS,
HUMMINGBIRDS AND JACKDAWS.
Listen at back at the cry
for SUPERNATURAL WORLD going by.
   Is everybody the carnival.

Is you and me group up TRAILING CAPES.
We group up STILTS AND SHADOW SHAPES.
Is we treble NINE MUSES
and group up BEST OF WITCHES.
Is you and me group up OGUN PEOPLE
and KRISHNA PEOPLE.
Look how she is ALL OF LEGBA
and he OUTRAGEOUS ROBBER.
   Is everybody the carnival.

Is you and me in a different glamour
raving with foreigner
like ANGEL OF PEACE
and she MEPHISTOPHELES
like he, a dull worker, is SOWER
and she, entrancing death, is REAPER.
Is you and me out of worlds
into worlds.
   Is everybody the carnival.

We group up a PHARAOH.
We group up SHANGO.
Look how whole of world, he's ATLAS
and she, falcon-faced, is HORUS.
Look at SWEETBOY FLIRT
and she, dripping jewels, is ALL OF WOMAN'S MIRTH.
Is you and me in a bacchanal
in a burru crowd jump-up for all.
   Is everybody the carnival.

Is we in loud horns and shouts
for GROUPS OF HARLOTS
with HERCULES AND HEBE
and ARISTOCRATIC ANANCY –
straight and round and round
through the town spellbound
in street
of music beat.
　　Is everybody the carnival.

Is you and me,
is we,
in sounds of RUM PEOPLE
and SUN PEOPLE,
in sounds of SUNFIRE
and sounds of SUKUYA,
in a trance of the dance,
we who'll never cut the raging pulse.

　　Is everybody the carnival,
　　everybody the carnival,
　　steel music, drumbeat.
　　Is we in the heat
　　revelling, having a shout,
　　in a break from day-in-day-out...

FIVE

Everyday Traveller

Taximan sees me today.
Sees me waving him down.
Again switches off
his FOR HIRE light.
Speeds up, passes me.

Similar. So similar
to our train driver
when he was late.
We passengers echoed
happy relief to see him.

Singled me out, at a glance.
Exploded in my face:
'You black bastard!
you keep your shit shut!'

On and on, on and on,
my ordinary face
confronts this
helpless defining
translated 'vulnerable'.

Late Stages of a Developing Man

This man feeling himself a ragged overripe man
living on nomansland
felt himself an overloaded anonymous man.

He examined himself and saw he was
a steady store-of-lacks man,
established as a big lacks-issuing man.

And knowing himself a failure-finder
man, grown into a fully loaded failure man,
he found an appeal-to man reinforced a failure man.

And puzzled how he was a well-schooled man
into being an unarmed target man
he saw only hiding eased him. And seeing

he'd developed into an attacks-attraction man,
all amazed how exclusions had set him up,
he felt betrayed how he was an agreed-on man.

And he was alarmed seeing himself
a public punchbag-man, for preconceived blows
as well as purely frustration blows.

And though this battered and stunted man,
this well drilled man in nonretaliation,
he noticed strange responses began to stir him.

And this wanting-to-be a reticent man
found in himself a strong having-nothing-to-lose
man, longing to be a big blows-trader man.

And though looking a shabby-seedy-sterile man
he'd become a ragbag of a passion
man, raging to be a hurt-celebration man.

He brooded on how everybody
took his head for a vacant big nought.
He caressed the hammer of his arm quietly.

And feeling he was no real poverty-stricken man,
only a man with lost value that'd make him rich,
he began turning flesh insideout for cash.

And now feeling himself a man participating,
he felt he worked at reclaiming
losses, by breaking skulls and jaws.

Feeling himself a sure-winner man, he stripped
petals like feathers fox-pulled.
He beat down gardens and girls and geriatrics.

Feeling himself a taught-to-be-an-ogre man
with beauty angled to avoid him,
he laughed in tearful faces.

Feeling himself more an unwelcome man,
more an uncuddled unreceived unsafe man,
he slapped backs with a weapon concealed.

And he didn't mind how he enlarged
as a magnet-for-malice man
and a mirror of grim-glances man.

And knowing himself more
of a questionmark man
he took to making entries with explosions.

And he called himself childless
though he had two children,
called himself motherless and fatherless

though his parents lived,
called himself alone, though he lived
often with armies in prison.

Millennium Eyes

We could never see enough.
We gleaned only a little of what is.
A hidden past little understood
a future view still out of sight
we could never engage with a full account.

Nothing outside was believable
as the image seen. Delivered words
carried omissions and additions
and stayed with closed faces
when seeing exactly was crucial.

And we yearned. We yearned to see
to the bottom of reasons,
through walls and over horizons.
We needed others to absorb that violence
in the seared flesh of our pain
and see our needs
and their rooted establishments –
see all of a situation,
all of an outcome
with all its angles, way back to source.

Now astrology tells us
the millennium brings new eyes:
make eyes, wear them openly, you grow
more and more eyes inwardly.
And colleges start up eyemaking courses –
a craze with students everywhere now.

In shades of grey, green and diamond,
brown, orange, blue, black and purple,
worn as pendants or bracelets
or as a band around the head,
eyes are the latest adornments.

Couples newly wed stare into
each other's manufactured eyes:
people say they see their future in them.
And crowned, bangled, garlanded, hung
with eyes, student groups go about singing
'More eyes, more eyes, more eyes!
The millennium brings new eyes!'

Words at My Mother's Funeral

(Maud Berry: 21.2.1897 – 10.7.1990)

While poinciana trees bloomed for sunlight
and mullets moved in the rivers,
unnoticed, quiet quiet you left,
completing footsteps and heartbeats
where ninety-three years halted.
And now, to your stay that marked us
we mark your going.
   O, mother, go well.

While sea waves rolled out on Fair Prospect beach
you vacated the house
in a silence at noon
ending a vessel that gave
one woman and five men
who in turn gave
their own little crowd you also mothered.
And we grew in your mothercraft:
your foodmaking, your sewing,
your artworks of hands and voices,
your touches now channelled under my skin,
your many pieces of songs in my head.
And I remember, you knew
when my tummy needed a rub
with the sign of the cross on it
and knew too when my tummy didn't really ache.
Like a season, you came to an end.
   O, mother, go well.

While a mongoose looked both ways to cross a track
you made your exit, but stay scattered
in memory, well highlighted, instinctive
and determined, to subdue and manage
each day's delivery of old losses not reckoned
in fresh nakedness, starvation, yelling
and accidents. Yet, with all the strength
of a horse in your mother-knowing
your sight became darkness
and your memory became confusion.

But hadn't you given yourself a patient daughter
to closely share your challenges and body pains?
Like a tree unfolding the sun's work
wasn't your giving your achievements
and your suffering an encounter you withstood?
    O, mother, go well.

While banana leaves and coconut limbs pointed
up towards the wide brightness
you left, where, so hard to win,
a strong heart prolonged you to endure
a new struggle of no-release
through months, weeks, days
when standing or sitting
like your lying down through all
the daylight and darkness was all agony.
Was this your purifying fire
that in waiting in the years before
had made you sing, over and over:
I will not let thee go Dear Lord;
I will not let thee go.
I will wrestle with thee till the break of day;
I will not let thee go?
    O, mother, go well.

While a woodpecker flew in a dipping flight
you made your departure.
Often, in these last years of pain
you remembered your husband
who'd gone before you thirtythree years.
But, always, your talk stayed
on your parents and your childhood home,
a place your yearning was fixed on.
And from the darkness, a streak of light emerged.
    O, mother, go full and free in love.
        O, mother, go well.

The Arrest

(on seeing Matisse's painting 'The Snail')

Green has a place like the heart.
More shapes of colours take
attention at the centre.
They look hung out like washing
of mostly handkerchiefs
in motion, going circular.

Underneath, a patch of white
is papered on like sky
on a base of sun-earth. Then
this level offers other happened
shapes. Like apertures or windows –
all views you would have
if flying, or crawling
or walking or standing still.

Now the colours are pools
of emotions – tones
that make an alphabet of moods.
They could be musical sounds
that left bodies of tones
and shapes in a precise order
but appear spontaneous.

You are toned up.
Sources are exposed here,
arranged, in these pieces
of colours these offsprings
of the sun, that have
their family difference richness.

An expanse of blue is meditative.
Strangely, an earthy-red becomes
a field like a vast bed.
You sense renewal
in a mask of sleep.
An awareness of purple robes
passes, like a breath-wave of wind.

The picture is a language.
It will not yield up everything.
You question yourself about
an interpretation of a coiled
movement. And, really, how
does snail-shell appropriate
such a range of tone?

You walk away. You wake up
in a warm rain. You see
that milked from sunlight
the pieces of colours are segments
hanging out a vision – a life's
circle that crept, into a spiral.

People with Maps

Unused, talents withered early
or were withering
going malformed in city slums,
in villages around shacks in drought,
in hunger, in loss of hope.

Street wandering, I walked into marchers
shouting 'Hurrah!' and blowing horns, beating
drums, and playing violins with announcements:
'Pains of nations united. All-nations'
abundance work declared!'

Impatient and confused, I rushed about asking
for more news. I am told, 'Visionaries are here
on the bridge, in sessions, with own teams.'

'Who are they?' I asked. 'Who are they?'
'Some heads of seminars are Tagore
and Matisse, Tolstoy and Mary Seacole,
Martin L. King, de Beauvoir, Fanon,
Leadbelly, Mozart, Montessori, Einstein.'

I ran to the end of the bridge where it opened
on to many roads. The heads of seminars had left.
Breathless I saw the new teams of people with maps.
They made notes of the many-pronged roadsigns:
to 'The University of World's Connection' villages.

Reply From Mother Africa

To your letter of outburst, your outcry
of spirit long overdue,
I will now reply.

Consider diverse difference. How movement
generates the many parts of life,
to release their own union.
And how trust is enshrined in oneness
undeniably. And your move
would observe trust. And time
for your ancestors' change had come.
             Consider.

Consider how a supplier –
like mountains of compost
like waterhole or loaded ship
or a calabash of fufu or wine,
serving birth, serving that
lonely loser, the bull elephant
consumed at the edge of the forest,
serving bleached grass brittly crackling
where dust sheets leap in dance
and, after August grazing pounded the grass,
November rains to water new growing –
how I facilitate.

I remember –
I watch migrating birds take off
and watch birds arrive.
I watch storks pick up lizards running away
from bursting fires under savanna sky,
watch a meercat stand erect on lookout duty,
other eyes watchful for movements
as finger-lipping rhinos pick leaves
and other square mouths firmly crop grass.
I watch zebras run with two-toed ostriches.
A lion hugging a zebra, kiss-capping its mouth
and nose. Monkeys find seeds, flowers,
fruits, birds and a baby gazelle.

I watch hunting dogs disgorge meat for puppies.
Watch a kissing bug suck a caterpillar dry
and a bird take the bug.
Round and round the zero hour,
I provide the means for meetings for movement,
not the movement itself.
Consider. Consider.

Consider how
the lion defines the zebra
as a meal to devour. Yet
wallowing in it and absorbing it
signals a compelling love,
a companionship in the flesh,
not a self-inspired love
but a driven and a violating love.

I remember –
a denial is a dispossessing,
a dispossessing is a devouring.

I remember –
a tribal will suggests
a possession of the whole world
alone, with only its own lookalikes.

I remember –
to be fixed within boundaries
for denial, you were renamed 'Negro'
and classified 'nonwhite', 'minority',
'underclass', 'ethnic', 'Third World'.
Consider your place, fully.

Consider –
in a dry season ever present
available pools and streams absent.
Faces released easily in symbolic light
add bars around faces in symbolic night.
An all-people network?
Hidden summers, hidden voices, in zero?
An all-human spirit inhabiting change?

I remember –
driven by dread
and violations and hidden compulsions
and lookalike self preferences,
like packs, like vultures, like prides –
round and round with the rotating sun –
movement is endless.

Reunion

Five hundred years
before reunion –
Mother Africa.

And here I am.
Here I am, where
at the beginning
one sun brushed me
in silence
and I became
obsessed lover of dance.

Here are these eyes,
these eyes around me –
unfathomable.

I do not know.
I do not know
one house
of my ancestral line.

I cannot grasp.
I cannot grasp
one word
in the voices I hear.

And yet
time has kept
every face my own –
every face my own, looking
like a house of exorcism, well lit.

Approach me.
Approach me
drums, whistles, chants.

I hear the time
of day one.

Reinitiate,
rededicate,
O all of me.

Reconsecrate my place
in every day:
valid like earth
with water
with sun
with air,
with one and every season.

I see
each different face,
like mine –
its own part
a symbol in a time
with its charge.

And, in me, at first:
I am a tree
never to be cut;
second: I am a word
reserved for ceremony;
third: I am a presence
never violated.

I am end.
I am beginning.
I am co-sharer.
I am a piece of the whole.
I am participator.
I am participator.

We dance.
We dance in dust.
We dance. We dance. We dance.

With found faces and drumming,
with found faces and drumming,
I am new spirit out of skin.
I am new spirit out of skin,
with found faces and drumming...

Contemplating Interdependence

As I breathe I try to remember
a crowded morning propels me on
from a birth from bruises and decaying flesh.

Wherever I arrive
I direct 'hello'
to mirrored images walking.

Before business I try to remember
my cellar under clearance

of blunt axes of haughty illiterates,
poisoned knives of shining graduates
and stolen jewels, guns and explosives.

Whenever I know I should exaggerate
I firmly pretend
I do not move with entanglements.

Before I curse I try to remember
not a nasty old day at all –
just a land-wash that splashed me.

I try to remember not to disguise
a bonding segment self
about partners' meetings
just like air or water rushing on.

Going About

I go in the belly of the running stream
and go in the feet of wind whisking by

I fly from where the road ended
and stay in footsteps gone

I go with the death dot of a flame
and stay with the last moment of the year

I go with sea wave into sand
and stay with day's merging with night

I search I search I search
where all times missed accumulate

SIX

FROM **CHAIN OF DAYS**

Ongoing Encounter

She said she called
in anguish, a wounder came
in a musical voice.

The blessing became a pain
manufacturer, the dazzling
face a death mask.

A rescuer came to her
loneliness, in a mood
lonelier than madness.

And desperate to forget,
she has a tormenting voice
that walks with her

unsettling her
in sullen helplessness,
preserving her like doom.

Insatiable Mover

Echoes pull echoes drive him:
    he'll have open smiles of green walks.

He insists from a fleshy womb and stands:
    he'll outdo the height of trees.

He wants a body agile and ageless:
    he feeds on flesh.

He wants the trees' deep singing:
    he settles himself within stripped wood.

He wants the splendour of petals:
    he wraps himself in colourful cloths.

He'll have the sun's dazzling scope:
    he hunts the ground and blood for gold.

He dreams of a devouring love:
    junction of a woman's thighs arrest him.

He'll have disembodied thoughts:
    words in print feed his insatiable eye.

He'll have the insides of mysteries:
    he breaks up air he exposes embryos.

He longs to manage an earthquake's might:
    he makes bombs make cities collapse.

He longs to escape from moods of melancholy:
    he lets music entrance him.

He longs to absorb length and breadth of the globe:
    he builds crafts and travels.

He longs to top up his height with stars:
    he reaches for the sky in a rocket.

He longs to draw on full depth:
   he goes down he sits in a pothole.

He longs for time gone and time to come:
   he sings he dances he laments.

He longs to confirm he grasps and wins:
   he flashes light he outpours darkness.

He'll have that answer that is absolute:
   he finds new ways to make disorder.

He'll have his voice collect all feelings:
   echoes pull echoes drive him.

He longs to beat all haunting:
   cessation takes over his limbs his lips
   his eyes his ears and stops his being.

Chain of Days

In the spicing the salting and the blackening
I'm poling up in fires of summerlight.
A tree blooms from my umbilical cord.
I look for a touch from every eye.
Darkness the wide shawl with sun's heat,
my mother's songs go from wooden walls.
Humming birds hovering
hibiscus nodding
I dance in the eyes of an open house.

On a summer road under swinging palms
a chain of days showed me bewildered.

Taking the drumming of the sea on land
I take the rooted gestures,
I take the caged growing.
Little lamps merely tarnish
a whole night's darkness.
Our stories bring out Rolling-Calves
with eyes of fire and trail of long chain.
I look for a sign in every face,
particularly in my father's face.

A joy is trapped in me.
Voices of rainbow birds shower my head.
I decapitate my naked toe.
My eye traps warm dust.
I'm born to trot about delivering
people's words and exchanged favours
or just grains of corn or sugar or salt.

Scooped water dances
in the bucket perched on me.
My bellows of breath make leaps of flames.
I muzzle goat kids in raging sunsets
and take their mother's milk in morning light.
Beaten there to remember I know nothing
I run to school with a page of book
and clean toenails and teeth.

All my homestead eggs go to market.
Farthings are the wheels that work my world.
My needs immaterial, I know I'm alien.

My father stutters before authority.
His speeches have no important listener.
No idea that operates my father
invites me to approach him.
And I wash my father's feet in sunset
in a wooden bowl.

And my father's toothless mother is wise.
My father coaxes half dead cows
and horses and roots in the ground;
he whispers to them sweetly and shows
the fine animal coat he persuaded to shine;
he pulls prized yams from soft earth
like big babies at birth
to be carried to rich tables.

Confused and lonely I sulk.
Companioned and lost I laugh.
I fill hunger with games.

On a summer road under swinging palms
a chain of days showed me bewildered.

I go to the wood
it is a neighbour.
I go to the sea
it is a playground.
I circle track marked hills.
I circle feet cut flatlands.

I turn rocks I turn leaves.
I hunt stone and nut marbles in woods.
I rob pigeon pairs from high trees.
Wasps inflate my face for a soursop.
I beat big nails into knives.
Tops and wheels and balls come from wood.
Yet movement and shape mystify:
I am tantalised.

I understand I'm mistaken
to know I'm truly lovable, and that
my lovable people are truly lovable.
I understand something makes me alien.
I wonder why so many seedlings wither
like my father's words before authority.

Wondering, dreaming, overawed, I sit
in the little room with faces like mine.
Low lamp light spreads a study
of the past on our faces.
I sleep with the purple of berries
on my tongue, and I warm thin walls.

On a summer road under swinging palms
a chain of days showed me bewildered.

I keep back the pig's squeal
or the young ram's holler
when my father takes out their balls
with his own razor.
Water I pour washes my father's hands.
I wish my father would speak.
I wish my father would use
magic words I knou he knows.
I wish my father would touch me.

Past winds have dumped
movements my ancestors made.
I dread my father's days
will boomerang on me.
I want to stop time and go with time.
In the hills alone I call to time.
My voice comes back in the trees
and wind. Why isn't there the idea
to offer me as sacrifice like Abraham's son?

My sister goes and washes
her breasts in the river.
Like a holy act I wash
in my brothers' dirty water.

On a summer road under swinging palms
a chain of days showed me bewildered.

My mother's dead granny brings
medicines to her in dreams.
My mother is a magician.
My mother knows how to ignore my father.
My mother puts food and clothes
together out of air. Bush and bark and grasses
work for my mother. She stops
the wickedest vomiting. She tells you
when you haven't got a headache at all.
In the pull of my mother's voice
and hands she stings and she washes me.

Put me in bright eye of sunlight
in shadows under broad hats,
on hillside pulling beans,
or chopping or planting,
I am restful with my mother.

The smell of sunny fields in my clothes
I meet my mother's newborn in the secret
birth room strong with asafetida.
I say goodbye touching my mother's mother
in the yard, her cold face
rigid toward the sky.

Quickfooted in the summer
I come over dust and rocks.
Echo after echo leaves me
from the edge of the sea,
from the edge of the sea.

Rolling-Calves: monstrous evil spirits, in the form
of calves, who haunt the countryside at night.

Stories by Bodyparts

1

I'm your breath-smell at waking.
I report your return from silence.
Use me in first kisses on children.
Use me in smiles on good-morning.

2

We are your eyes, your windows
on altitude and depth.
on faces hiding messages.
Sometimes we see
elevations unite levels.
Usually, horizons are fixed.
Blood boils us often
more than curved hips.
Bareness calls down hoods
yet you want to see the loving
next door: we wonder
what bird could be singing.
We wonder, to whom
could we expose we care.

3

We are your feet. We rubbed
away your baby tantrums
into leg-shapes of clockhands.
We stand at doorways:
no last abode anywhere.
Obsessed with wings, you make us
go about in traps.
We climb we fall.
We linger it hurts.
If you laugh or kiss, always
we are way at the end.
We dash for the bus, your
destination's eyes, high up
at its rear, laugh at us
and disappear. Then at last

we face outwards, like
clothes-irons rested
going colder and colder.
We see: no bath was ever able
to soak away our travels.

4

I am your hand. I hang
lightly or become a stone.
Agent of eyes and heart
I pull triggers.
I stroke up love.
I wrap up weapon.
Good cash or bad or its absence,
all arrive for pocketing.
And as this ladling palm, I take
a nail driven through me.
But like a leaf, I wave,
I shiver,
I shrivel,
I slip away.

Notes on a Town on the Everglades, 1945

Sounds of 'Ma Baby Gone'
make the ghetto air in blues
in this Southern town.

It charges me with dread
with puzzlement with wonder
at this haunted mass of black people.

They hum the blues in shanty streets
and open fields. They dance the blues
in bars. They pray blues fashion.

They gesture and move and look
like refugees or campers on home ground,
or just a surplus of national propagation.

And fenced in, policed, blues-ridden,
the people plant wounds
on any close body it seems.

Women and men, all ages, go and come
in bandaged movements
like hospital escapees.

And on the compelling side,
the gleaming nearness of town,
the bridge is policing.

White men through their streets,
like white men in the fields,
are knowing and proud stalwarts.

With cold eyes like passionless gods
their groomed bodies go
extended with guns.

An Arrested Young Man's Reply

In shadows of backs turned
my muscles grew

In manhood unreachable
I absorbed

In noises of attack
my manhood overtook me

Captivated by what I have
I strolled the centre of town

Detention and Departure

I shouldn't live, you know, man.
I shouldn't live,
too much hunger devoured me,
too many lacks hit me in
and stamped me down
all heels over head long long time.

I washed up here washed-up,
an overdone case, man,
rolled from ship of fire,
tongue clipped,
steps short.

A dry stick sun-charged man,
I powered axe,
powered crowbar and hoe,
I flattened hills.
I made mountains make valleys.
I banked back all of the sea this side.

Then turned into a bottomless bag, man,
I swallowed up all the sea-sound.
I saw I sucked in the force of the sea.

I lifted, man,
lifted up,
dropped off white bones like shell.

I climbed this high noon, man,
climbed this high noon,
hands sharp,
sharper than steel,
head big,
loaded with eyes.

I took this high noon, man,
took this high noon,
in claim of all earth,
in claim of all earth, man.

New World Colonial Child

I arrive to doubtful connections,
to questionable paths,
to faces with obscure
disclosures, with reticent
voices, not clear why
my area is inaccessible,
my officials are not promoters.

Odd farthings drive the circles
bare, around the houses, like
goats tethered and forgotten.

I can't endure like my father.
I wait bowed. I wait
in rain-saturation,
in sunlight-dazzle.

Dark valleys and snow domes
are elsewhere. I am a piece
of disused gold mine, sometimes
a feather of shot game, other
times a seedbed of obsessions.

And making it is making.
Who isn't faced
to surrender money or knowhow,
surrender strength or bold,
reluctant or benevolent blood?

In the haughty handling
winners keep a military stance.
Avenues were never landscaped
for people blueprinted for rags.

A meeting has stayed
on a footing of war,
levels of weaponry unknown:
words misstate manoeuvres.
I hide. I admit
at best I am stubborn
like weeds on a path.

Absence of a choice has
a grasp of a slow death.
Absence of a hero makes men
headless, makes world-successes
work from failed retaliation,
And who shall expose
the virtues of difference?

Father's learning long taught
him, he's too lazy
to be man, too worthless
to be paid for work. He walks
like a loaded donkey,
unqualified to engage
essential listener. He knows
knowledge inflates a person
beyond little speeches in fragments.

I cannot assess my father.
I do not know what makes him
history. He's merely our
mystery of helplessness,
our languagemaster dumb
with forgetfulness, our
captain without compass.

And I cannot fathom
the people he's given me.
I still have to see if
our failures opened
inner doors of a meeting,
behind netting jaws, more firmly
than pain or profit.

I do not know my kinspeople
to be less than I know them,
yet judgements make me
feel they are less.

I do not know my losses,
I only sense them. I
do not know any licence
against me, it only seems so.
But a rope at my neck is
a shame I am born in
that I can't understand.

I hold on to a pride:
I own a map
underfoot. I own a king
and kingdom and robes
and rites I use.

On May 24 every year
I march, in fresh khaki shorts.
We wave the flag. I
with my slave scars march
and sing: Britons never,
never, shall be slaves.

In my dumbness I know
in our sky-wide gestures
gentle strengths arouse
a light in everyone.
How can I say what best
my heritage surrendered?

How can I know my voice
isn't the grunt of a pig,
isn't the squawking of a goose,
or the howling of wind?

A colony is a lair
of a country found. New lords
give names to people and places
and things and stamp them.
Equal terms would hold
a more-than-equal people
to a gunless robbery.

A colony has no resource
value for itself. A colony
never redeems itself with payment,
it merely receives.

A colony is given freedom,
when freedom has always been there.
A colony is given
Independence, when independence
can only be arrested.

Without plan or invitation,
like a season impels
I am charged to move.

I leave the encampment.
Like fresh awakening
I emerge round corners.
And again a different
weather is fierce
and I freeze-burn.

How shall anyone agree
a colony-native isn't
a colonised ghetto captive?
How shall we
clear away old orders?

On an Afternoon Train from Purley to Victoria, 1955

Hello, she said and startled me.
Nice day. Nice day I agreed.
I am a Quaker she said and Sunday
I was moved in silence
to speak a poem loudly
for racial brotherhood.

I was thoughtful, then said
what poem came on like that?
One the moment inspired she said.
I was again thoughtful.

Inexplicably I saw
empty city streets lit dimly
in a day's first hours.
Alongside in darkness
was my father's big banana field.

Where are you from? she said.
Jamaica I said.
What part of Africa is Jamaica? she said.
Where Ireland is near Lapland I said.
Hard to see why you leave
such sunny country she said.
Snow falls elsewhere I said.
So sincere she was beautiful
as people sat down around us.

In-a Brixtan Markit

I walk in-a Brixtan markit,
believin I a respectable man,
you know. An wha happn?

Policeman come straight up
an search mi bag!
Man – straight to me.
Like them did a-wait fi me.
Come search mi bag, man.

Fi mi bag!
An wha them si in deh?
Two piece of yam, a dasheen,
a han a banana, a piece a pork
an mi lates Bob Marley.

Man all a suddn I feel
mi head nah fi me. This yah now
is when man kill somody, nah!

'Tony,' I sey, 'hol on. Hol on,
Tony. Dohn shove. Dohn shove.
Dohn move neidda fis, tongue
nor emotion. Battn down, Tony.
Battn down.' An, man, Tony win.

Two Black Labourers on a London Building Site

Been a train crash.
  Wha?
Yeh – tube crash.
  Who the driver?
Not a black man.
  Not a black man?
I check that firs.
  Thank Almighty God.
Bout thirty people dead.
  Thirty people dead?
Looks maybe more.
  Maybe more?
Maybe more.
  An black man didn drive?
No. Black man didn drive.

Letter to My Father from London

Over the horizon here
you say I told you
animals are groomed like babies
and shops hang wares
like a world of flame trees in bloom

Lambs and calves and pigs hang empty
and ships crowd the port

You say no one arrives back
for the breath once mixed becomes
an eternal entanglement

You say unreason eats up the youth
and rage defeats him

Elders cannot be heroes
when the young wakes up centrally
ragged or inflated on the world
and the ideal of leisure does
not mean a bushman's pocketless time

An enchanter has the face of cash
without sweat
and does not appear barefooted
bursting at elbows and bottom

He has the connections and craft
to claim the sun in gold
and the moon in diamond

You cannot measure the twig-man
image you launched before me
with bloated belly
with bulged eyes of famine
insistent from hoardings and walls
here on world highstreets
holding a bowl to every passerby

You still don't understand
how a victim is guilty as accomplice

Island Man

How I have watched you chop and ruffle
a tired face of land with hands
like dead roots, at full life
keeping back weeds
from a hillside patch.

How I see winds molest
your rags rotten with sweat,
see the sun paint you deeper and deeper
and suck your bosom dry.

Man grilled in sunken eyes,
minder of bush knowledge
the wind laughs at repeatedly,
knocking down your sticks,
beating up your few hills of yam,
I have watched you, seen you
stumble to shadows
reckoning insensibly
the season's and land's potential.

A new and clean voice burdens you:
your eyes hide from the meeting,
your humbled smile trembles with fear,
your arms are restless
like wild wings of a seized bird.

Unable to go any other way,
object of a landscape,
you lift weighted feet
with the memory of chains
in floods and arid ground:
your shoulder rocks a dirty bag,
your stumpy machete in your grasp.

Between bamboos and old palmtrees
you are in pursuit,
making me know I see a man
loaded in mind, but only
with the ways of his woods
that exclude him
and control him by compulsive tracks,
by strong sunrise
and its last rage of departure.

Luckless man of ceaseless attempts,
I have known you and watched you.
I watch you closer
now, watching myself.

Fantasy of an African Boy

Such a peculiar lot
we are, we people
without money, in daylong
yearlong sunlight, knowing
money is somewhere, somewhere.

Everybody says it's a big
bigger brain bother now,
money. Such millions and millions
of us don't manage at all
without it, like war going on.

And we can't eat it. Yet
without it our heads alone
stay big, as lots and lots do,
coming from nowhere joyful,
going nowhere happy.

We can't drink it up. Yet
without it we shrivel when small
and stop forever
where we stopped,
as lots and lots do.

We can't read money for books.
Yet without it we don't
read, don't write numbers,
don't open gates in other countries,
as lots and lots never do.

We can't use money to bandage
sores, can't pound it
to powder for sick eyes
and sick bellies. Yet without
it, flesh melts from our bones.

Such walled-round gentlemen
overseas minding money! Such
bigtime gentlemen, body guarded
because of too much respect
and too many wishes on them,

too many wishes, everywhere,
wanting them to let go
magic of money, and let it fly
away, everywhere, day and night,
just like dropped leaves in wind!

African Holiday

(for Nelson Mandela in prison)

A strange wait
how leaders rot
swishing flies

A strange decay
of presence
walled up with words

A strange cancellation
of arrival
and promises

A strange mission –
tomorrow's news gone
like rolling waves arrested

A strange departure
of voices
a place developed

A strange reversal –
offering death
life's prime giving

Thinkin Loud-Loud

Yu sen fo we to Englan, she sey.
Yu buy de house.
Yu buy de car.
We inside dohn roll fo food.
I expectin yu numba 6 child.
Why yu beatin out yu brain on books
wha tight like a rockstone?
Find teacher. Find teacher, she sey.

Gal, I sey, fifty year I walkin earth:
ow can I mek a teacher wise
ABC still a-puzzle me?
Ow can I show we own boy an girl dem
words on me eye put up high wall?

She sey, yu sign yu name wid X.
Yu show no paperwork, but
yu av yu workins
wid pencil an paper in yu head.

Gal, I sey, dat worded page
is a spread of dead tings: insect dem
wha stares at me
doing notn sayin notn
but turn dark night
an bodda me an bodda me
fo dat time I hear print a-talk
like voices of we children.

Last Freedom of Martin Luther King

Who is here without grief?
Who cannot share
our fruit of death fallen before us?

In the secrets air and clay emphasise in blood,
winding rivers do not mourn
in processions of children, men, women.
We have roads endlessly.

Only last night I looked on your living face;
a man unafraid in deadly shadows.
Today your exit dims a world.

You who returned no blows,
you who would undamn abundance,
you who would see enslaver and slave released,
you who would let illusion fade,
you who would arouse new day from wreckage,
you who would cut roads of diamond in city jungles,
you who in all this make us mourn.

O enemies are defined,
madness is courage.
A dead past animates us,
our ghosts insist.

And dream of brotherhood fixed your eyes.
Agonies of silent people lit your thoughts.
Citizens' birthrights must not be bargained.
'We Shall Overcome' moved, like moving
hives of bees behind you,
along the longest highways.

You linked people whose visions
were intolerable. You engaged the trapped
and hungry and quickened them, releasing
a new selfknowing like fire.
Yet in the middle of a beginning
we mourn you here and our innocence.

Our Love Challenge
(for Mary)

Maybe designs for conflict worked me
when I exploded on the stage
with slave anger
thoughtless you'd walk out wounded

So full in time I let out
my raging hungry dogs
who threatened me

You take it I accuse you
of seizing children's keep
with whip with cruel lordship
you say I invest in vengeance
I storm you with ancestors' sins

You cut all lines to me
you go to old fires behind barriers
I like an outlaw withdraw

But alone again leaving
tiger and lion interlocked
we go slowly

We exhaust suppositions
we become this new area
between killing sun and killing ice

Statue, Paul Bogle, Jamaica

New form on my eyes.
Cut down man is mounted.
The embalmed has unclothed
a figure of flame!

Go easy on me.
We were similar men –
of the same allegiance,
the same yearnings –
to unfetter a finite face.

Hold me.
But let me measure my pace.
Impulses you store
consume too much.

You moved
for my release.
You died.

Torchlights have marked
your angles
among chains and wrecks.

Hold me in failed words
and failed sinews and blood
and burning thoughts.
Hold me in our pain.

Erected from oblivion
you are awesome here.

Sunlight reveals you
anew. Registering me
in faces of blooms.
Instead of denial, dispossession, death.

I Spoke Severely

I spoke severely to my hands
for the chains
that contained my steps
    I go vigilant for the hold
    of invisible chains

I reproached my voice
for the silence
that silenced me
    I go vigilant for a loaded voice
    laden with silence

I scolded my being
for movements in the time
that arrested me
    I go vigilant for a full time
    that is not free time

I centred my mind
to dispel the surrender
that dominated me
    I go vigilant
    renewing my mind
    with constant eyes
    with constant eyes.

It's Me Man

I wouldn't be raven
   though dressed so
I wouldn't bleed my last
   though crushed
I wouldn't stay down
   though battered
I wouldn't be convinced
   though worst man
I wouldn't stay pieces
   though dissected
I wouldn't wear the crown
   though king of rubbish
I wouldn't stay dead
   though killed
I wouldn't stay dead
   though killed

Dogwood Tree

Topping your stance here,
dark green – a waver,
yet, beaten shaped,
clung-to by vines
and rammed with limbs.

You have been sawed and chopped.
Parts gone as shafts of carts
and tools and fence posts that grow.

And you try to overcome
your stumps. I stroke
your straight wood.

I want to know.
I want to know how
you took your incentive
in delight in the sun's eye
and your unyielding character.

I want to know if you are
an impulse or an echo
that became this old iron tree
and medicine tree,
with a juice of bark to make
a toothache stop
and make fish rise
and float sideways?

Going with All-Time Song

Say
Goodmorning Love
in the midnight our market

Say
Yesterday showed
our yearbook of yearning

Today washes
the words and eyes
in wonderment

Say
Tomorrow is the torch focussed
now is my noontime

in the waking
     singing singing
I AM IN LOVE

Just Being

I laughed and my echoes shook apples
off trees of a thousand lands

My swimming trailed one long lonely road
all deep in the sea

I stepped out and stood on a mountain top
high up in a sheet of sunlight

A Woman Reflects

A stepping back not offered,
time folds up its tracks
with actions of light and darkness
into layers of memory.

And with the travel not noticed,
with its drama scarcely appraised,
at this place today,
a beginning is staged.

A changed past becomes
new brute life
in a formed bridge to food
and the outlook.

Behind are the burnt out
and closed pathways,
the mummified things
with some not quite lifeless.

Then towards one's restful dawn,
a stranger like gnarled sticks comes
and shouts up the household,
announces Good Morning and sits.

And behind a hassle today
the heirloom ring is sold
towards leper-care. Old pictures
and a tapestry go for skeletons.

Other women sit in doorways.
Some encircle offices. All say
they'll release armies
from hypnotised killings.

Yet, old flavour of teatime
is sadly mixed with new
prayer mutterings on the air
and government cannot act.

What conviction could have been seen
as pain circulated? Could
my coat have stayed mink's,
and not a lady's best garment?

From Lucy: Englan a University

Darlin, you did ask a good question.
You know, and I know, how white folks
can go on, bout they need a holiday,
and manage get it cross
they 'adventurous', they 'curious',
and land up in Africa
and India and China, etcetera, etcetera.

Well, darlin, Westindians come
get known as travellers for food
and clothes: not folks who did long
to feel somewhere else,
long to touch snow with eyeball,
and all curious too to see
horseback lords at home, at fireside
maybe thinkin how they did long
for company of bushman, and did long
to take in sounds
and feelin's of jungle places.

And all in all, sweetheart, though
our move was blind date to Mother
Country, it look now it did carry
far-sightedness. And I swear
heavn did know something bout it.

Darlin, when real person get seen
in black figure, like when real
human get known in white figure,
is celebration, is teatime all roun,
or rum and blackcurrant. And still
I get surprise, when I see
somebody posh behavin like
a hungrybelly in we distric there.

And real news this, me dear!
From distric there, another
barefoot boy is makin mark.

Fool-Fool Boy-Joe son come get degree,
education degree here in London:
and Bareback-Buddy is teacher now.
Bareback teachin. He teachin
black and white children mix together.
Leela, you see how what
you don know is older than you?

Sweetheart, we mus remember you know
how ol people did say, 'Man is more
than a flock of birds.'

Benediction

Thanks to the ear
that someone may hear

Thanks to seeing
that someone may see

Thanks to feeling
that someone may feel

Thanks to touch
that one may be touched

Thanks to flowering of white moon
and spreading shawl of black night
holding villages and cities together.

Inward Travel

Weighted by exhaustion
today, I have no eyes outward.

I have become a log
reverting through green.

I ascend with rivers' faces
till again together I am

a drifter stilled, a raft
losing weight steadily

absorbing light's clarity
in expansive quiet.

Silence is hynoptist.
Magnitude washes

me in nothing. Then,
I see I have returned

in slow turn of a wheel
quickening.